# Inspiring Independent Learning

## Successful Classroom Strategies

# Inspiring Independent Learning

## Successful Classroom Strategies

MARY ANN RAFOTH

The Inspired Classroom Series

NEA PROFESSIONAL LIBRARY

## ADVISORY PANEL

**James Duggins**
Professor of Education
San Francisco State University
San Francisco, California

**Arlene Dykes**
Third Grade Teacher
Disnard Elementary School
Claremont, New Hampshire

**Thomas Ousley**
Director of Attendance
Jennings School District
St. Louis, Missouri

**Melissa W. Earnest**
History and Political Science
Teacher
Caldwell County High School
Princeton, Kentucky

**Rosalind Lucille Yee**
Reading Specialist
Prince George's County School
System
Annapolis, Maryland

Copyright © 1999 National Education Association of the United States

Printing History
  First Printing: June 1999

ACID FREE
∞

PRINTED WITH
SOY INK

**Library of Congress Cataloging-in-Publication Data**

Rafoth, Mary Ann.
    Inspiring independent learning: successful classroom strategies
    Mary Ann Rafoth.
        p.   cm. — (Inspired classroom series)
    Includes bibliographical references. (p.  ).
    ISBN 0-8106-2954-2
        1. Independent study. 2. Educational tests and measurements.
    I. Title.   II. Series.
    LB1049.R35   1999
    371.39′43—dc21

                                                            99-24013
                                                            CIP

# Contents

# *Preface*

I wrote this book for teachers and support personnel who want to help students learn *how* to learn but do not want to turn every class into a study skills lab. *Inspiring Independent Learning* provides practical examples of embedded learning and study strategies that really work for students. The strategies are easy to implement and, in most cases, build on what is already happening in the classroom. The strategies draw on my experiences as a former teacher and school psychologist and my recent work with classroom teachers from kindergarten through grade twelve. All of the strategies in this book represent success stories used by teachers and support teams in real classrooms.

## HOW THIS BOOK IS ORGANIZED

The role of the teacher in inspiring independent learning changes as students' metacognitive knowledge (their knowledge of their own learning and memory processes) develops. For this reason, Part I begins with an overview from a developmental perspective that speaks to classroom teachers, curriculum directors, school administrators, and support professionals working to help every student succeed in the regular classroom. Chapters 2, 3, and 4 describe specific strategies in the primary, intermediate, middle, and secondary grades that inspire student learning and increase the likelihood that students will learn independently in the future.

Part II looks across grade levels at how educators can assess and improve upon students' independent learning skills through interviews and follow-up interventions, peer tutoring, and portfolio assessment. Chapter 5 introduces the Metacognitive and Study Skills Interviews, two tools that can help teachers and support personnel gain insight into an individual student's or an entire class' knowledge of learning strategies and application of study skills. Case studies provide examples of how these assessments can be used to identify and remediate study skills deficits and will be very helpful to instructional support teams, guidance counselors, special educators, and school psychologists. Appendices A and B contain the interviews, scoring directions, student profile forms, and a menu of interventions that address the issues identified through the interviews.

Chapter 6 reviews a program that trains peer tutors to act as study skills coaches to students identified as "at-risk" for failure in high school. Appendix C contains a copy of the manual used to train the tutors in the Share the Secret Program, in which peer tutors "share the secret" of their academic success with their assigned students. Finally, Chapter 7 outlines a model for assessing whether or not students have acquired strategic learning skills through performance evaluations and student portfolio products. The chapter includes checklists, reproducible activities for helping students learn, and suggestions for assessing their mastery of independent learning skills.

## HOW THIS BOOK CAN HELP YOU

*Inspiring Independent Learning* seeks to help teachers and other support professionals enhance their students' ability to achieve through subtle changes in instruction that support the development of independent learning skills. Again, all the examples and recommendations are proven winners that are easy to implement and shown to improve student performance. By being more effective in teaching students how to learn, we can help them become more effective students.

# *Acknowledgments*

I would like to thank the many dedicated teachers in the Blairsville-Saltsburg, Leechburg, and Gateway School Districts in western Pennsylvania, who shared their successful strategies for independent learning with me over the years I worked with them. In particular, I would like to thank Dr. Terry Foriska, whose leadership in the Blairsville-Saltsburg and Gateway School Districts allowed for rich consultative experiences. In addition, I would like to acknowledge the many other teachers I have met through my classes and other in-service activities. They, too, have shared their skills and experiences with me.

I particularly wish to thank Diane Stipcak. Her clerical assistance ensured the completion of this book in a timely manner. Finally, as always, thanks to Ben, Henry, and Paige for their love and support.

# PART I

# *Effective Strategies by Grade Level*

# CHAPTER 1

# Overview: The Teacher's Role in Inspiring Independent Learning

## SUCCESS STORIES

Teachers can inspire independent learning through easy, often subtle, techniques that gently place responsibility for learning in the hands of students and teach students how to help themselves learn. The techniques vary by grade level. None is overly time-consuming, and each technique leaves students with a skill or strategy they can apply in future situations to foster independent learning. For example:

- When a kindergarten teacher wanted to ensure that students knew basic information such as the days of the week, calendar months, and spelling of basic colors, she used songs and rhymes to help her students encode the information. But more important, she taught them that making up songs and rhymes helps them learn. Soon, her students had mastered the information and were demanding new songs and rhymes to help them with new lessons.

- A teacher of second and third graders, who were struggling to read and master vocabulary, introduced a five-step study method, as described in Chapter 2. The method initially took extra time for the students to do, but it was time well invested. Within a month, the students were spending less time studying their words than before using the five-step method and, for the first time, successfully retained their new words.

- To introduce story problems, a teacher of third and fourth graders showed students how to identify three different problem-solving strategies, as described in Chapter 3: personalization, visualization, and algorithms. Students practiced each strategy and then chose one that they found most helpful. When faced with future problems, these students have a template of solution strategies. Not only do they have a sense of which strategy works best for them, but also they have "fallback" strategies on which to rely.

- A middle school teacher found that students were failing quizzes on vocabulary assigned from a literature-based reading program. After several weeks of exhorting students to use study sheets containing the words, definitions, and sentences from the book, the teacher tried a new technique, as described in Chapter 4, which combined individual and small group review. Quiz grades shot up, and students began recognizing the vocabulary words in other contexts.

- A tenth-grade math teacher became frustrated at students' poor note-taking skills in her math classes. When she gave them a structured set of guidelines for how to take and use notes, as described in Chapter 4, quality improved dramatically. Similarly, another high school teacher who was discouraged by poor class participation found the level of participation greatly improved when he taught students to monitor the quality and quantity of their own involvement. Quiz grades and confidence also improved as student participation increased.

# CRITICAL CHARACTERISTICS

In all of these situations, with guidance from the teacher, students assumed responsibility for their own study and learning. Because these strategies enabled students to succeed, their motivation and confidence rose. The teachers spent less time nagging, chiding, and feeling discouraged over student failures. As straightforward as most of the strategies described above are, they share some critical characteristics of strategy instruction that must be adhered to in order for students to adopt strategies and generalize them to future learning situations. These critical teacher behaviors are essential for success. Moreover, the role teachers play in enhancing independent learning changes as students develop cognitively.

*Primary Grades*

At the primary level (grades K–2 or ages 5–8), children's ability to control their strategic behavior is limited. They have difficulty focusing and maintaining their attention without guidance and cannot direct themselves to engage in learning strategies. Typically, young children do not have an accurate sense of the limits of their memories and use only repetition, often ineffectively, as a memory aid. It would be unrealistic to expect young children to independently generate strategies, generalize strategies from one situation to another, and monitor their learning. Within these limitations, however, teachers can enhance strategic skills for independent learning in the primary grades by building on what they are already doing. For example, kindergarten and first grade teachers often teach songs and rhymes to children to aid recall. Teachers typically group or chunk information and create sufficient rehearsal activities in the classroom to guarantee retention. When the first structured study activities are introduced, such as spelling tests, teachers often suggest that words be written or reviewed a fixed number of times (for example, "Write each word five times."). They do not anticipate that young children will know how to effectively study, so the students are told specifically what to do.

While these activities help children learn, alone they do not enhance independent learning skills. To foster independent learning in the young student, teachers must *overtly* tell students about strategies and point out their effectiveness. In other words, the teacher must inform students about strategies while modeling, such as in the following example:

> Mrs. Rivera wanted to help her children learn the calendar months. She taught them a song to help them remember and told them that songs and rhymes help memory. Before rehearsal, she cues the children, "What's a good way to remember important things?" They answer, "Sing a song." She then asks, "Do we have a song to remember the months?" As the children sing, she comments, "the more we practice the better we'll remember."

Teachers must use the strategy in other contexts and overtly point it out to students. For instance: "You're having trouble spelling your last name? Let's make a little song from the letters! It will help you learn the letters just like the calendar song helped you learn the months." Teachers using these strategies in the primary grades have observed that young students see the value in them and often will ask for information to be put into a song or rhyme format. They have observed students using a song or rhyme in other recall situations (Rafoth 1995).

Children in the primary grades should begin to engage in activities that lead to later self-evaluation and monitoring, even though they are too young to do so effectively on their own. Often these activities rely on peer checks, which teachers can work into a classroom routine through a specified "checking" activity after the completion of a task. For instance, one child can check to make sure another child followed the teacher's directions and wrote the spelling word "three times."

In summary, in the primary grades, the teacher should overtly inform students about strategies, model and carry them out, and structure classroom routine to include simple self-checks and peer review.

## Intermediate Grades

As children move into the intermediate grades (grades 3–5 or ages 9–11), they become more capable learners. Metacognitive skill, or the ability to direct cognitive processes, begins to emerge (Flavell 1992). For example, children will often spontaneously chunk information before rehearsing it and can often accurately estimate the amount of information they will be able to recall easily (about seven units). They more easily recognize the value of study strategies and become more efficient at rehearsal. They can engage in self-testing strategies with direction, although they often will not immediately recognize "out of the ballpark" or obviously incorrect answers.

In the intermediate grades, the teacher must still inform students about strategies and overtly model them. At this level, students should first practice strategies provided to them by the teacher and then try to generate some simple strategies on their own. Self-monitoring and evaluation activities can be successful if they are highly structured and often demand peer involvement. Peer editing, for example, works well in grades three through five. At these grade levels, peers can be used to help students make the transition away from dependence on the teacher toward more independent learning (Palinscar and Brown 1984).

In summary, in the intermediate grades, teachers should suggest and model more complex strategies, help students begin to generate their own simple learning strategies, and introduce methods in which peers can play a role in independent learning.

## Middle School

The teacher's role in fostering independent learning in students at the middle school or junior high level (grades 6–8 or ages 12–14) is particularly critical. These students are metacognitively able to begin directing, monitoring, and evaluating their own learning, yet few students display these skills because teachers rarely teach or reinforce them. Teachers often assume that middle school students know how to study. Cues to study often consist of vague

reminders to "study for the quiz" or "review the notes." Sometimes teachers actually discourage activities that lead to more active, independent learning.

For instance, in a recent observation, a seventh grade student asked a teacher about the amount, type, and content of an upcoming test:

> "How many questions will we have? Will they be multiple choice or fill-in? Will the test cover our book and our lab?"

These are excellent questions and indicate the student was beginning to think about how and what to study in preparation for the test. Unfortunately, the teacher replied, "That's for me to know and you to find out!" This response effectively extinguished these good strategic behaviors in this student and probably his classmates as well.

Teachers must help middle school students move into independent learning while providing the structure necessary to help them succeed. Middle school students are ready to use more sophisticated strategies for effective independent learning, such as assignment books, note-taking systems, study plans for tests, and elaborative memory aids like mnemonic systems. Teachers must present these skills across contexts and reinforce them throughout the curriculum in order for effective learning and skill generalization to occur.

In summary, at the middle school level, teachers should not only supply this kind of strategic information to students, but they also should ensure that students ask for these skills and reinforce them appropriately.

## High School

In high school (grades 9–12 or ages 15–18), the teacher should continue to model and reinforce strategies for effective independent learning and help students recognize and develop a personal study style. In high school (and in many middle schools, as well), students change classes throughout the day and may have from four to eight core teachers. Often, these teachers assume that students already

have study skills or will pick up any deficient skills through a study skills class. However, high school teachers must help their students learn by *embedding* effective study approaches within the context of the content area they are teaching, rather than relying on imparting independent learning strategies through a *detached* format, such as a study skills lab.

To enter post-secondary education as efficient independent learners, students must be able to choose strategies that work for them in particular contexts and use systems for learning and studying they find effective (Weinstein, Zimmerman, and Palmer 1988). They must be able to monitor and evaluate their own learning. Because exams and other formal performance measures occur less frequently in high school and in post-secondary education, students must know how to study in a distributed fashion: at regular intervals rather than just the night before a test.

In summary, at the high school level, teachers must ensure that their students have developed a personal study style that works well for them and can focus on self-monitoring and distributed study.

## SUMMARY

Teachers play an important role in enabling their students to develop independent learning strategies, often by imparting simple strategies that can easily be embedded into the classroom routine. They must be aware of what students can and should achieve at different metacognitive stages in their lives. The strategies that students learn in the upper grades are inherently more complex than what they can master in the early grades. However, these more complex strategies are based on the recitation and other simple strategies they have learned as younger students. Finally, teachers must take particular care not to discourage the kinds of questions and activities that help students become independent learners.

# CHAPTER 2

# Primary Grades: Building a Strong Foundation

Children in the primary grades depend on their teachers for guidance, structure, and direction in learning. Teachers can help students gain confidence and take responsibility for their own learning by teaching them how to:

- use simple memory strategies
- follow directions
- use comprehension strategies
- monitor learning

These strategies should help students achieve the independent learning outcomes listed in Figure 2.1 by the end of the primary grades. To help students achieve these outcomes, the teacher needs to inform students about the strategies, model and carry them out, and structure classroom routine to include simple self-checks and peer review.

## SIMPLE MEMORY STRATEGIES

By first grade, children understand that repetition enhances their memory. However, they cannot monitor when to end

## FIGURE 2.1
### Independent Learning Outcomes
### for the Primary Grades

Primary grade teachers worked with the author to create the following list of independent learning outcomes that students should achieve by the end of the second grade.

1. Students will demonstrate the use of rhyme and song to enhance memory for key information. (Application)

2. Students will state the relationship of rhyme and music memory (for example, "a song or rhyme helps you remember something."). (Knowledge)

3. Students will demonstrate important cues to understanding and remembering oral information (for example, use of pictures, questioning, and ordering steps in directions). (Application)

4. Students will use checksheets and partner checks to aid in monitoring their own performance. (Application)

5. Students will demonstrate questioning to enhance understanding with a teacher and a student partner. (Application)

6. Students will demonstrate verbal and nonverbal cueing of steps when repeating directions as an aid to memory (for example, labeling "step 1, step 2" or using a color to mark a particular step, such as green to signify addition). (Application)

7. Students will identify personalization as a memory aid and demonstrate its use on a memory task. (Knowledge and application)

8. Students will demonstrate visualization by drawing a picture or image to help them remember something and state that making a picture in your head helps you remember. (Knowledge and application).

9. Students will demonstrate organizing information or objects into groups (with teacher direction) and state that finding likenesses helps in remembering. (Knowledge and application)

10. Students will demonstrate efficient rehearsal techniques and check retention of material with a model or partner. (Application)

rehearsal to ensure retention. They profit from other memory strategies carried out for them by teachers (for example, learning the alphabet through the ABC song), but they do not realize that such strategies enhance memory. They cannot usually generate strategies independently.

However, young children can learn more efficient rehearsal strategies and ways to make connections between activities and purposeful strategies to increase memory. The use of song and rhyme is one of the best ways to increase memory in young children. Key to the successful use of this strategy in the early grades is the overt connection *by the teacher* of the song or rhyme to enhanced remembering. Teachers must tell students the connection and reinforce it across contexts in order for children to gain an understanding of the strategy, to realize how and why it works, and to increase the likelihood that they will generalize it as more mature learners. A sample teacher-student dialogue might sound like this:

**Teacher:** Who knows their ABCs?

**Students:** (many raise hands)

**Teacher:** Great! Who can tell me one thing we did to help learn our ABCs?

**Student #1:** We wrote the letters!

**Student #2:** We practiced them.

**Teacher:** Good! How did we practice them for fun?

**Students:** Sing the song?

**Teacher:** Yes, we sang the song—the song makes it easier to remember and more fun to learn. We need to learn our colors and we need to learn how to spell them. How can we make that fun and easier?

**Students:** Make a song?

**Teacher:** That's right. We can make a song!

Let's start with a song about the color RED, R-E-D. Making up a little song about something you remember is a great way to learn.

(Teacher demonstrates song and informs students when they are successful that the song helped them remember.)

Song and rhyme can teach students such key information as the spelling of their names, their addresses and phone numbers, color words, alphabet letters and sounds, numbers, important classroom rules and directions, and basic math facts. Teacher-made songs and rhymes can be personalized to increase effectiveness, or teachers can draw upon published songs and rhymes. (The Reference list suggests several sources.) Again, it is essential that teachers overtly and repeatedly tell children that song and rhyme will help them remember and cue the children to use them. These messages will lead students to generalize the strategies to new situations as they mature metacognitively.

## FOLLOWING DIRECTIONS

The first step in following directions is learning to listen to them. In the primary grades, children begin to use cues to understand and remember oral information and directions, such as using pictures, questioning, and ordering steps in directions while listening. To promote selective attention—the skill of attending to essential or important information—teachers can hold group discussions following oral reading or content presentations. In these discussions, children raise their hands and tell one relevant fact or make one statement about the topic. *Before they can make their statement, they must first repeat what the previous child said.* Another technique is the 30-second "listening list." In this activity, children close their eyes for 30 seconds and then list all the sounds they heard.

Students can practice comprehension monitoring through activities that require them to listen for missing information. After listening to a brief list of instructions, they can say what else they would need to know to complete an assignment. After hearing a short story or mystery, they can state what additional information they would need to know to predict what might happen next. In order for these strategies to work, the teacher must first model examples and, again, overtly work through the thinking process. If students have difficulty identifying what is missing from a set of instructions, for instance, the teacher can act out the

directions so that what is missing becomes obvious.

Other strategies for helping children learn to self-direct while following directions include teaching cue words for problem solving and introducing mnemonic pictures. For example, students can learn to recognize cue words for addition and subtraction that can be encoded with mnemonic strategies. ("All," "altogether," and "and" suggest addition.) Estimation strategies allow children to make predictions about problems' solutions and to check their accuracy. Teachers must build checking strategies into the classroom routine for young children to adopt them. For example, teachers may want students to learn to check subtraction by adding. They can have the students work in pairs so that each student takes turns being the "checker." Or they can incorporate checking into worksheets and assignment forms as shown below:

1. 796      check:       2. 356      check:
   -421            +___          -221            +___
                    796                            356

Consistent color coding of important information and direction words also helps direct selective attention. Teachers can write or underline new words or concepts in a different color than surrounding information. For math problems, they can always write the word "add" or a "plus sign" in green, "subtract" in red. "Greater than" and "less than" signs are much easier to remember when coded green for "greater than" and red for "less than." Students can color code an arithmetic worksheet themselves before they begin to solve problems. In spelling, words can be color coded to emphasize letter patterns. Teachers can mark beginning sounds, vowels, or endings with specific colors or with italicized or underlined type:

Spelling list:   h*itch*
                 w*itch*
                 s*titch*
                 d*itch*
                 p*itch*

# COMPREHENSION STRATEGIES

Children in the primary grades need guidance from the teacher to learn how to understand what they are seeing or hearing. Illustrations of spelling words often help them learn meaning and recall the correct spelling, especially when they draw their own pictures. Other visual strategies can aid comprehension by depicting relationships. Even kindergarten students successfully use "webbing" techniques to show connections and examples. A typical activity might involve a letter or letter grouping at the center of a piece of paper, surrounded by pictures cut from magazines or drawings of words that begin with that letter or sound. Building on this technique, first and second graders can organize information in concept webs after a lesson or unit. Webs in the primary grades are initially teacher-directed and may include both pictures and words. By the end of first grade, however, children often produce their own webs by working in pairs and using large pieces of paper spread on the floor. These webs can serve as their "notes" when orally summarizing and writing about the topic.

Venn diagrams aid children's conceptualization of relationships among characters, events, and objects. At first, the teacher needs to establish the desired organizational structure with the students and point out its worth. Similarly, story maps organize and increase students' comprehension and retention of important points.

Many teachers use cued steps to aid students in learning to write letters. They encourage children to subvocalize the cued steps when writing. Thus, the letter "a" is remembered by first drawing the apple (circle) and adding the stem (straight line). The letter "b" is cued by first writing the bat (straight line) and then adding the ball (circle). These series of cued steps teach writing within a meaningful (and therefore memorable) context. They are especially helpful for students who are having trouble with particular letters.

When introducing new concepts or procedures, teachers should present only one example at a time so children do not become distracted. Teachers can model sequential steps in problem solving and overtly acknowledge their thinking

processes when approaching a problem for the first time. To increase comprehension, teachers can also carry out or prompt learning strategies for a student. When the teacher carries out the strategy, the student can devote the entire short-term memory space to processing the new material. For example, when a child is reading and comes upon a new word, the teacher can re-read aloud the previous words in the sentence to give the child context clues about the word to be decoded. This makes available to the younger student a strategy normally available to older, more competent readers.

Previewing material also fosters processing of information in short-term memory. Teachers can identify difficult or new words that students will encounter prior to a reading selection and have the students define, decode, and use the words in a sentence. When one teacher had difficulty getting her students to remember vocabulary words by studying lists, she had them take a more active role through the five-step method illustrated in Figure 2.2.

A simple previewing method is to direct students to look over their material before beginning to read or work. For students who have difficulty previewing, teachers can provide copies of the material for the students to mark with a highlighter and can point them to targets such as chapter titles, subheadings, and captions that are appropriate for preview highlighting.

Students can also work in pairs to question each other about the main idea of a story (characters, problem and solution, setting) after listening to or reading a story. Students in the primary grades often require concrete anchors, such as different colored cards to wear around their necks, to remember their roles. For example, a red card indicates that a student is the "asker," and a green card indicates he or she is the "answerer." After exchanging comments, each pair formulates an opinion about what will happen next in the story. The teacher can then direct students to ask themselves the same kinds of question when reading alone. Reciprocal reading techniques developed by Palinscar and Brown (1984) utilize a similar approach by asking students to take the role of the teacher and to think of questions a teacher might ask.

## FIGURE 2.2
## A Vocabulary Process Strategy

For each new word, the student goes through the five steps described below. At first, it takes students up to five minutes for each word. Soon, it takes them less than two minutes and their retention of the word improves significantly.

| | |
|---|---|
| 1. **DECIDE** that you want to learn about a word(spelling, definition). | 1. (Students write their responses in this column.) |
| 2. **FIGURE OUT** what the word means by:<br>• context clues<br>• word parts<br>• asking another person | 2. |
| 3. **VERIFY OR FIND OUT:**<br>• dictionary/glossary<br>• parent/teacher/classmate<br>• cluster/similar words | 3. |
| 4. **CREATE A MENTAL PICTURE:**<br>• what feelings does it make you think of<br>• see word (spelled correctly)<br>• say the word | 4. |
| 5. **SHOW YOU KNOW:**<br>• think of similar words<br>• create a sentence using the word<br>• write a definition in your own words<br>• draw a picture of the word or something that reminds you of the word | 5. |

# MONITORING LEARNING

A teacher can encourage independent monitoring of memory and learning through the use of checksheets and partner checks prior to teacher evaluation. Figure 2.3 illustrates self-check forms developed for use in a physical education class. Teacher demonstration and classroom participation can also foster rehearsal strategies for remembering. To teach how to spell a word, for example, a teacher can demonstrate rehearsing the letters aloud and writing the word several times on the board. The children can then model the teacher by reciting the letters as a class and writing the word several times at their desks. When instructing children in rehearsal, teachers should follow procedures that promote the maintenance of these strategies. They must tell their students that using this strategy will improve their task performance and point out when children's performances have improved by working with a partner. They can also suggest that students use rehearsal strategies to learn other information, such as arithmetic,

---

**FIGURE 2.3**
**Self-Monitoring Form for Physical Education**

- Hop 5 times on your right foot.
- Hop 5 times on your left foot.
- Jump with both feet 5 times.
- Leap landing with your right foot.
- Leap landing with your left foot.

| Check the correct box. | Able to do: | Needs work: |
|---|---|---|
| 1. Hopped 5 times on your right foot. | | |
| 2. Hopped 5 times on your left foot. | | |
| 3. Jumped with both feet 5 times. | | |
| 4. Leaped landing with your right foot. | | |
| 5. Leaped landing with your left foot. | | |

---

and demonstrate and remind students of the strategy and its benefits until the strategy is well learned.

Children can also begin monitoring their own performance by predicting how they will do on successive rehearsals in a learning log:

## Math Facts Log

**Student:** Carrie Rodriquez
**Week of:** January 5

| Math facts | Number correct | Prediction for next day |
|---|---|---|
| Monday | 15/20 | 18/20 |
| Tuesday | 17/20 | 18/20 |
| Wednesday | 19/20 | 20/20 |
| Thursday | 19/20 | 20/20 |
| Friday | 20/20 | 20/20 |

Teachers should model and emphasize to children that they must constantly self-monitor by checking after *each* verbalization or writing to make sure their rehearsal is accurate. As most teachers know, it is not unusual for a young child to turn in a page with a spelling word written incorrectly 10 times! Teachers should also monitor to make sure that children do not use rehearsal in an inefficient manner. For instance, instead of writing the entire word, some children write the first letter of a spelling word 10 times down the page, then the second letter 10 times, and so on. This is *not* an effective learning method.

Teachers can introduce rehearsal routines that help children and their parents. In fact, parents are often unaware of efficient rehearsal techniques and need clear, brief instructions from the teacher to help them with their child.

Teachers can also combine a "sandwich drill" with mnemonic and monitoring techniques to enhance rehearsal in reading vocabulary. In this drill, a small number of unknown words (20 to 30 percent) are sandwiched between a list of known words (70 to 80 percent). When specific unknown words are especially difficult, some children benefit from mnemonic aids (*Saturday,* like the planet *Saturn,* is an example of one student's suggestion). Some children may learn by singing difficult words (*Wed-nes-day* spells Wednesday). Others will benefit from visualization.

# SUMMARY

The many strategies described in this chapter help students in the primary grades learn self-direction. Teachers play a vital role in introducing the strategies in an age-appropriate context, repeating the strategies until they are well understood, and overtly stating the role of the strategies to their students. Habits begun in the primary grades become the foundation for later independent learning.

# CHAPTER 3

# Intermediate Grades: Increasing the Role of Peers

The intermediate grades (grades 3–5) are key years for embedding independent learning skills because students are beginning to develop metacognitively (Bruning, Schraw, and Ronning 1995). Teachers can foster independent learning skills in these grade levels to help students practice:

- elaborative memory strategies
- organizational skills
- reading comprehension
- problem solving
- monitoring learning

These strategies should help students achieve the learning outcomes listed in Figure 3.1 by the end of the fifth grade. Teachers of intermediate level students must still do a substantial amount of modeling and overt discussion of the strategies. Peers also become more important in helping students in the transition away from dependence on the teacher toward more independent learning (Palinscar and Brown 1984).

## FIGURE 3.1
### Independent Learning Outcomes
### for the Intermediate Grades

Intermediate grade teachers worked with the author to create the following list of independent learning outcomes that students should achieve by the end of the fifth grade.

1. Students will use a variety of elaborative memory strategies to enhance recall in core subject areas such as spelling. (Application)

2. Students will use several methods of organizing data, such as concept webbing, mapping, or basic outlining. (Application)

3. Students will record assignments on a daily basis and indicate completion and difficulty level. (Application)

4. Students will identify basic strategies for reading comprehension (previewing, questioning, clarifying, and summarizing) and demonstrate such a process (as in reciprocal teaching). (Knowledge and application)

5. Students will monitor their learning by engaging in pre-testing with a partner across several subject areas. (Application)

6. Students will monitor writing assignments by editing each other's work and revising appropriately. (Application)

7. Students will engage in basic self-evaluations of their work, for example through checksheets and ratings on accuracy and neatness. (Application)

8. Students will use "notes" in the form of concept maps or outlines to write or present orally to the class. (Application)

9. Students will engage in prediction and estimation as a form of monitoring in reading and math. (Application)

10. Students will identify and use three problem-solving strategies: personalization, visualization, and algorithmic solutions where appropriate. (Knowledge and application)

# ELABORATIVE MEMORY STRATEGIES

Techniques to help students develop elaborative memory strategies in the intermediate grades include the use of visual imagery; rhyme, music, and raps; acronyms and acrostics; and association strategies. Common spelling mnemonics include acrostics that help students remember how to spell complicated words *(arithmetic: A rat in Tom's house might eat Tom's ice cream)*. Division acrostics *(Does McDonald's sell cheese burgers*: divide, multiply, subtract, check, bring down) remind students of the correct way to compute more advanced math problems. Acronyms are also helpful and popular with students this age (*HOMES* to remember the Great Lakes: Huron, Ontario, Michigan, Erie, and Superior).

Because students at this age are concrete thinkers, they will particularly remember acrostics and acronyms they generate themselves or that involve their classrooms, classmates, or teachers. Raps can help them remember basic math, the states and capitals, or other facts. Visualization and word play, in which students draw pictures to illustrate their spelling words, help many students remember. Teacher-generated songs aid students in recalling the organization of a book, parts of speech, or other information.

By increasing the ease of retention of rote information, elaborative strategies allow students to feel in control of their memory and empowered as learners. They feel successful and will apply these memory strategies in later independent learning situations if they are prompted to use them and made aware of their utility.

# ORGANIZATIONAL SKILLS

Intermediate grade students can learn to organize data through such methods as concept webbing, mapping, and Venn diagrams. These organizers can be used after class discussions, oral teacher presentations, or independent reading. Students can learn to use other types of graphic organizers to help them process and identify specific kinds

of concepts or information. *Again, it is essential that teachers stress the reason why different organizers are used.* For example, to help students order information in sequence, a teacher could present a simple prompt:

1._____
2._____
3._____

To help students arrange events in a causal relationship, a prompt like the following is helpful:

_____          _____
(cause)          -------->          (effect)

_____
(effect)

A graphic organizer like the following is useful to help students compare and contrast data:

Likenesses:

_____<—-> _____
_____<—-> _____
_____<—-> _____

Differences:

_____ ////_____
_____ ////_____
_____ ////_____

To help students conceptualize a problem, solution, and result, an organizer like the following would help:

Problem: ———>   Solution: ———>   Result:

Using visual imagery can also teach students to organize different writing conventions. For example, a drawing of a person can illustrate the five parts of a letter, from the top of the head and mouth (heading and salutation) down to the feet or signature. The classic three-paragraph essay is easier for students to compose when they first complete a graphic organizer like the one shown in Figure 3.2.

Students should begin keeping brief assignment sheets or books in the intermediate grades that record subjects, assignment directions, and due dates. Monitoring and

organizational skills are also facilitated when students rate their assignments from hardest to easiest in order to direct their attention to how much time each assignment will take. In the intermediate grades, teachers must model good assignment recording—and even tell students exactly what to record. Students can trade assignment sheets and check each other's recording for accuracy.

| FIGURE 3.2 Graphic Organizer for Student Writing | | |
|---|---|---|
| Generalization | | |
| Paragraph Idea 1 | Paragraph Idea 2 | Paragraph Idea 3 |
| Restatement-Conclusion | | |

# READING COMPREHENSION

Students deepen their understanding of reading comprehension strategies in the intermediate grades. Working in small groups or with partners to check for comprehension allows students a transition from teacher dependency to independent learning. Basic strategies that students should learn to identify and use include previewing, questioning, clarifying, and summarizing. Again, because children are concrete thinkers during these grades, techniques that personalize reading or allow them to take on roles facilitate comprehension. For instance, Figure 3.3 contains a format for students to summarize key information from stories by pretending to be newspaper reporters. Simple formats are useful to organize book reports, especially oral reports. The teacher prompts students to search for the essential information they should capture: for example, the title and author, main characters, setting, plot, and resolution.

## FIGURE 3.3
### "News Reporter" Summary Sheet

**GIVE US THE SCOOP!**

DIRECTIONS: Read the story or article. On the lines below each question, write your answer. If the answer to a question is not found, write "Not Given" on the line.

Who?    What?    When?    Where?    Why?    How?

_____  _____  _____  _____  _____  _____
_____  _____  _____  _____  _____  _____
_____  _____  _____  _____  _____  _____
_____  _____  _____  _____  _____  _____
_____  _____  _____  _____  _____  _____
_____  _____  _____  _____  _____  _____
_____  _____  _____  _____  _____  _____

REPORTED BY _____

Students in the intermediate grades often find that story maps, such as those in Figure 3.4, are useful tools in aiding comprehension. This strategy helps them to analyze the text by defining the story in terms of setting, characters, problem/goal, major events, and resolution. Even younger children can demonstrate their comprehension of a story by illustrating these structural elements. Story maps allow for different points of view and encourage students to think about problems or events they feel are most important.

# PROBLEM SOLVING

Students in the intermediate grades are ready to expand their menu of problem-solving strategies. One method of efficient problem solving involves teaching students to use *estimation* to rule out obviously incorrect answers. When children in the intermediate grades make computation errors, they are often outrageously inaccurate. Teachers should introduce estimation through easy-to-compute

## FIGURE 3.4
### Two Story Map Formats

Title of Story          Characters          Setting

_____    _____    _____
_____    _____    _____
_____    _____    _____
_____    _____    _____
_____    _____    _____

Problem          What Happened?          Solution
                                         (At end of story...)

_____    _____    _____
_____    _____    _____
_____    _____    _____
_____    _____    _____
_____    _____    _____

At the beginning of the story...

Then...

At the end...

problems. As with other strategy instruction, teachers should first model estimation and then gradually let students carry out the procedures independently. Other experiences with numbers will help students improve their estimation abilities. For example, teachers can relate

estimation to shopping, reminding students that they have less money after a purchase. From there, they can point out that in solving a subtraction problem, the answer always has to be less than the initial sum.

Three problem-solving strategies introduced effectively to students in the intermediate grades are personalization, visualization, and algorithmic solutions. Through personalization, the teacher presents examples, explanations, and problems in a format that is personal to individual students. Personalization not only increases children's interest, but also activates appropriate mental images or mental sets for understanding. Teachers must initially personalize lessons for students, but, eventually, students can work through "personalization routines" on their own. For example, a standard math problem might read:

> Jack had 45 crayons to divide among six of his friends. How many crayons will each friend get if he divides them evenly? Will any crayons be left over? How many?

To personalize the problem, the teacher replaces Jack's name with one of the student's names, and replaces crayons with something the student has and may want to divide among friends:

> LaToya had 45 "beanie babies." She had six friends over to her house and wanted them to each play with the same number of beanies. How many beanies will each friend get to play with if she divides them evenly? Will any be left over for LaToya to play with? How many?

The problem instantly becomes more relevant, more concrete, and more solvable. To teach students to personalize their own problem, teachers can develop a "fill in the blank" format (such as the following) once students are familiar with the process:

> (Write your name) had 45 (write a favorite toy or candy). (He or she) had six friends who all wanted to (play with

them or eat them). How many (write the toy or food you picked) will each friend (play with or eat) if (he or she) divides them evenly? Will any be left over for (write your name)? How many?

Visualization is a second good problem-solving strategy for students at this age. Visual images help to make problems concrete and bring them from the realm of the abstract to the student's real world experience. Drawing a picture helps some students determine what information they have been given in the problem and what information is relevant to the solution. For example, if the problem is to determine how long it will take to drive from City A to City B at 60 miles per hour, some students find it helpful to draw the points on a map, the road, and the car.

For many students at this age, a third strategy—recognizing algorithmic solutions—is an effective way to problem solve. An algorithmic solution is a step-by-step procedure for finding a solution to a problem with a fixed answer. Teachers can show students that certain words (such as "how far" or "how long") serve as clues to what kind of computation is required. For students who have difficulty recognizing the clue words that help to determine the kind of problem and the appropriate solution set, prompt cards are helpful.

Students at this age have spontaneously developed many problem-solving strategies on their own, yet they may be unaware of these activities as learning strategies. Teachers should be on the lookout for these independent learning strategies, however simple they seem. They might include counting from one addend until the second amount is reached, repeatedly adding figures to solve multiplication problems, using hatch marks, basing their answers on already-solved related problems, and overlearning basic facts until they're automatically recalled. Students who engage in such strategies spontaneously are developing metacognitively. The more they are aware of the strategies they currently use, the more likely they will be to adopt more sophisticated ones.

# MONITORING LEARNING

Although teachers often tell students to "check" their work, students often do not understand the methods that allow them to do so or why it is important to use these methods. Teachers need to model self-checking strategies and provide students with the rationales that explain why these strategies work. Increasing students' computational accuracy increases the likelihood that correct mathematical facts will be stored in long-term memory. After completing an assignment, students may check their computations with a calculator, recompute the problem, or engage in a related operation (e.g., using multiplication to check division).

To monitor spelling progress, teachers can write or have their students write the week's words on index cards, spelling some of the words correctly and some incorrectly. Students can then test themselves to see if they recognize whether or not the word is correct. Or teachers can have their students copy spelling words on a piece of paper with a dotted or folded line down the side. The children practice each word by quietly saying and spelling it aloud and then closing their eyes and spelling it aloud again. They fold the paper so they cannot see the word, write it, and then unfold the sheet to check if they spelled the word correctly.

Peers can help with these various checking strategies. Another area where peers can be quite helpful in monitoring performance is in writing. Peers can effectively edit each other's written assignments if they work within a well-established classroom routine. For example, Figure 3.5 provides an excerpt of a third grade teacher's "buddy edit" rules.

Students at this age often rely on partners (classmates or parents) to quiz them, but this is a critical time for students to begin developing self-testing strategies. Through self-tests, students learn when to terminate study and what needs additional review. They can also engage in basic self-evaluations of their work. For example, they can complete checksheets and forms that rate their accuracy, completeness, and neatness. One teacher had students complete a "responsibility graph" in which they graphed how frequently they

---

### FIGURE 3.5
### Buddy Editing Rules
#### (Using Peers To Monitor Work)

1. React with a compliment!

2. Suggest an improvement:
   content
   logic
   use edits
   give harsh feedback in a *kind* way
   (not "This is boring!" instead "This seems average.")

3. Check spelling and punctuation.
   (put a check mark by it)
   (put a question mark if unsure)

4. Buddy signs work! (make the changes your buddy suggests)

(Teacher should still follow up with all students.)

Source: Dr. Ray Beisel, University School, Indiana University of Pennsylvania, Indiana, PA

---

completed a series of flashcard drills and homework assignments.

## SUMMARY

Teachers of third through fifth grade students play an important role in introducing more sophisticated learning strategies than students could handle in the primary grades. Providing students with concrete examples enhances their ability to learn spelling, math, and other subjects. By introducing monitoring and other methods that involve peers, teachers are helping students on the path to independent learning.

# CHAPTER 4

# *Middle and High School: Developing Lifelong Habits*

The middle school grades (grades 6–8) are critical years for acquiring learning strategies. Both the curriculum demands and expectations for independent learning increase and place additional academic pressures on students. Similarly, in high school (grades 9–12) students are expected to know how to study and to develop a personal "study style" that will allow them to succeed in post-secondary settings and to learn on their own as adults.

As students develop metacognitively, they are more able to use independent learning strategies. However, many middle and secondary level students still need help from teachers in developing the skills necessary for academic success. Teachers can help students in these grades develop strategies in five main areas:

- elaborative memory strategies
- organizational skills
- reading comprehension
- critical thinking and problem solving
- monitoring learning

# FIGURE 4.1
## Independent Learning Outcomes for Middle School

Middle school teachers worked with the author to create the following list of independent learning outcomes that students should achieve by the end of the eighth grade.

Outcomes 1–6 can be taught through a detached study skills, reading, or learning strategies class and followed by embedded reinforcement in content areas.

1. Students will list and explain several organizational strategies. (Knowledge/comprehension)

2. Students will list and explain several methods of increasing reading comprehension. (Knowledge/comprehension)

3. Students will describe a basic outline form of note taking and list the types of information important to record, ways to abbreviate information clearly, and the types of cues teachers give to students to help them note important points. (Knowledge/comprehension)

4. Students will define "monitoring learning" and give examples of how they might predict an exam grade, know when to reread material, and know when to stop studying for a test. (Knowledge/comprehension)

5. Students will explain several different mnemonic techniques including chunking, association, and visualization. (Knowledge/comprehension)

6. Students will identify a compare/contrast model to analyze two different points of view, documents, or events. (Knowledge/comprehension)

Outcomes 7–14 *must* be taught within the content areas.

7. Students will demonstrate effective use of organizational strategies through the use of an assignment book and specific planning strategies. (Application)

8. Students will demonstrate the effective use of at least one strategy to enhance comprehension with a text or other assigned reading. (Application)

9. Students will complete notes in a basic outline format with teacher guidance. (Application)

*–continued*

10. Students will demonstrate the use of self-testing through accurate test grade prediction and test preparation strategies. (Application)
11. Students will demonstrate effective use of mnemonic techniques while studying. (Application)
12. Students will explain several methods of problem solving and demonstrate effective use of each in mathematics, science, and social studies. (Application)
13. Students will list ways to prepare and take a test and demonstrate effective test preparation (for example, through use of study card clusters). (Application)
14. Students will use a compare/contrast model to analyze different viewpoints, documents, or events in English and Social Studies. (Application)

These strategies should help students achieve the learning outcomes listed in Figure 4.1 by the end of middle school and Figure 4.2 by the end of high school.

# TWO APPROACHES TO INDEPENDENT LEARNING

Schools often attempt to teach learning skills through a study skills course or lab or a reading skills course that is *detached* from the rest of the curriculum. These detached courses are usually ineffective because students rarely generalize the skills to their actual coursework. They may memorize a few strategies in an abstract way, but gain little unless such skills are cued and reinforced in the context of the rest of the curriculum. (Gettinger and Nicaise 1997). In contrast, an *embedded* approach is more effective: students learn study skills within the context of the regular curriculum as they master new concepts, acquire information, and learn other skills (Jones, Slate, Blake, and Holifield 1992).

Embedded strategy instruction is much more likely to occur at the primary and intermediate levels, when children typically have one to three core teachers and often

## FIGURE 4.2
## Independent Learning Outcomes for High School

High school teachers worked with the author to create the following list of independent learning outcomes that students should achieve by the end of the twelfth grade.

1. Students will demonstrate use of individualized assignment books and other organizational strategies for long-term projects. (Application)
2. Students will recognize different patterns of text organization and describe the implications of each. (Knowledge/comprehension)
3. Students will demonstrate several ways of organizing and improving memory with content material. (Application, Knowledge/comprehension)
4. Students will demonstrate an effective method of personal note taking, including elaboration in preparation for testing. (Application)
5. Students will demonstrate study plans for different types of exams and list a repertoire of test-taking techniques. (Application)
6. Students will demonstrate flexible reading rates for different types of reading material and for different purposes. (Application)
7. Students will demonstrate problem-solving strategies across content areas and in varied contexts. (Application)
8. Students will develop a personal study style consistent with their individual learning style. (Application)

study different disciplines through thematic units. The acquisition of basic skills (reading, writing, and basic computation) also lends itself to inclusion of other intellectual skills (problem solving, learning strategies). In middle and high school, however, students often have from four to eight core teachers, and faculty members tend to be more oriented within their own academic disciplines. Teachers often assume that students already have independent learning skills and expect to refine thinking skills and focus on

discipline-related concepts and information. Thus, embedded strategy instruction is not as frequent or consistent.

A combination of these two approaches, embedded and detached, can be effective at the middle and high school levels. Students can learn various strategies and learning systems in the abstract, saving time for the content-area teacher. However, it is crucial that skills are embedded into the content areas and reinforced. This chapter first describes how teachers can impart embedded strategies and then recommends techniques for making detached study skills courses more effective.

# ELABORATIVE MEMORY STRATEGIES

Students in middle and high school have developed the metacognitive skills to benefit from elaboration techniques to aid memory. As they were for intermediate-level students, acrostics and acronyms are good ways for adolescents to encode important facts they will continue to use in later life. For example, they might learn the Geologic Time Scale through an acrostic: _Can old senators demand more powerful positions than junior congressmen?_ (Cambrian, Ordovician, Silurian, Devonian, Mississipian, Pennsylvanian, Permian, Triassic, Jurassic, Cretaceous, Tertiary, and Quaternary). While younger students remember more when they use elaborations given them by teachers, older students learn and remember more when they use elaborations they have created (Pressley, Borkowski, and Schneider 1987). Thus, students often have more success when they make up and use their own acrostics and acronyms. Like their younger counterparts, they need to see how memory strategies improve their recall and result in better grades to generalize their use.

Teachers often anticipate that students in middle and high school will have efficient rehearsal routines, but many do not (Schneider and Pressley 1989). Many older students remain locked into the "magic number" strategy they learned as younger children. Because young children do not have the metacognitive ability to monitor their learning and determine adequate study and rehearsal time,

teachers typically instruct students to carry out an activity a fixed number of times. For example, first grade teachers often tell their students to write each spelling word three times. Many students then equate studying with a fixed number of rehearsals and, as they mature, still do not develop self-testing and other efficient strategies for independent learning. Thus, they may write each vocabulary word three times in eighth grade and stop studying. They may read over their history notes three times in eleventh grade to prepare for a test. They do not know if mastery has occurred but they say they are "done studying" after a fixed amount of rehearsal. Instead, middle and high school teachers might suggest a step-by-step plan for distributed study, as illustrated in Figure 4.3, in which students study in small amounts of time throughout the week, rather than all at once. The plan could be applied to other content as well.

---

**FIGURE 4.3**
**Card Cluster Strategy for Distributed Study of a Social Studies Assignment**

- Write what you want to remember (date, name, term, vocabulary word, etc.) on the unlined side of an index card.

- On the other side, write the event that matches the date, term, or word definition and who the person was.

- Study by placing the cards into three categories:

    1) Mastery—the cards you know immediately.

    2) Part Mastery—the cards you need just a little more practice with.

    3) No Mastery—information you do not know or got wrong.

- Review the "part" and "no" cards frequently for about 10 minutes at any one time. Use bus time, homeroom time, and other "odd" times in the day for review until all the cards are in the "Mastery" pile.

---

# ORGANIZATIONAL SKILLS

To enable students in middle and high school to work more independently, they must be directly taught organizational skills. Students in middle school often need help as they make the difficult transition from elementary to middle or junior high school. Many have a locker for the first time, with very little time between classes to go to the lockers to retrieve the materials they need. Strategies such as PREPARE are excellent supports for students when they begin middle school:

**P**lan locker visits: "When can I go to my locker?"

**R**eflect: "What you need to get?"

**E**rase personal needs: "Do I need to use the restroom?"

**P**syche yourself up for class: "What is my goal for my next class?"

**A**sk where the class is going: "What are we supposed to do today?"

**R**eview notes and study guides: "What did we do in the last class?"

**E**xplore the meaning of each class: "What am I supposed to learn?"

Students also benefit from assignment books, but the teacher cannot simply hand them the books without guidance. Ideally, the students were gradually introduced to the use of assignment sheets or books in the lower grades. Whether this has occurred or not, students need feedback about the accuracy and thoroughness of their record keeping. Teachers usually do not have the time to check assignment books regularly, but peers can check each other through an assignment book swap. After peers check each other's books, the teacher can easily identify students who are in need of individual monitoring.

Note taking is another organizational skill students are expected to develop in the secondary grades. Students can

try different methods of note taking in study skills classes or within another designated course, but they need to develop an effective personal style and understand the basic goals of note taking in their different courses:

- to record main ideas

- to record supporting detail

- to note important examples or illustrations

- to save time through the use of abbreviations and "shorthand methods

- to create a permanent record for later referral and study

The best way for students to understand these basic goals and to adopt behaviors that facilitate their attainment is *for the teacher to model note taking*. Teachers can model note taking on the chalkboard or with an overhead projector. At first, teachers must overtly indicate to students why they choose to write down certain points, how they organize information, and how they use abbreviations to save time. Providing students with brief outlines with blank spaces (skeletal outlines) also facilitates learning to take notes. When teachers model note taking, students are able to observe content-specific skills in taking notes. For example, a tenth grade math teacher who wanted her students to develop a notebook for later use provided specific instructions, as shown in Figure 4.4. She found that the students' note-taking skills improved, as did their performance in class.

Ideally, students should realize that note taking is a form of elaboration on what is learned as well as a memory aid. However, they must be taught how to highlight, code information, and add to their notes. Students learn how to do this best when their teachers actively model strategies for manipulating notes, such as when they underline, use different color chalk, label information as important, indicate examples by circling or boxing them in, and use asterisks or stars to direct attention to important points.

Students must also receive feedback about their note-taking skills. They need feedback both in how well they initially take notes and in how well they manipulate and

## FIGURE 4.4
### Note Taking in Mathematics

How to use your notes to prepare for a math test:

1. Identify the type of problems that will be on the test. (If you are not sure ask the teacher!)

2. Find the section in your notes that covers each type of problem. You should have written a heading at the beginning of each day's notes.

3. Read through your notes and rework the examples step by step. Highlight or underline main headings and important information. Put a star next to or a box around examples. Add extra notes of explanation where needed.

4. If there is something you don't understand in your notes, find the section in your textbook and read it over. If you still don't understand something, check with a classmate or your teacher.

5. Once you think you understand the examples in your notes, make new practice problems up and see if you can work them, following the same procedures as in the examples in your notebook.

6. If possible, exchange practice problems with a classmate. Check to make sure you both come out with the same answers!

If you are permitted to use your notebook during a test, follow these same procedures during the test, using the test questions where the new practice problems are. Of course, omit Step 6—no checking with a classmate—but do check your own work on a test.

review notes prior to a test. Teachers may feel that they do not have enough time to review notebooks on a regular basis. Instead, they can introduce a format in which peers check each other's notebooks. Teachers can easily scan these checksheets and identify students whose notebooks require more careful perusal.

## FIGURE 4.5
### Notebook Swap

Trade notebooks with another student. Use the questions below to check each other's notebook.

Student: _____

Reviewer:_____

Date: _____

|  | YES | NO |
|---|---|---|
| Are the day and the date noted? | ___ | ___ |
| Are all examples numbered and copied? | ___ | ___ |
| Do notes have main and subheadings? | ___ | ___ |
| Is there white space around notes? | ___ | ___ |
| Has important information been written down next to examples? | ___ | ___ |
| Has important information been underlined or highlighted? | ___ | ___ |
| Are examples starred or boxed? | ___ | ___ |
| Have other notes been added to class notes? | ___ | ___ |
| Is handwriting neat and readable? | ___ | ___ |

Ultimately, note taking is a decision-making process that increases learning and retention of material, so it is important for teachers to emphasize personal decision making in taking notes (Bretzing, Kulhavy, and Caterino, 1987).

# READING COMPREHENSION

Students in middle and high school are expected to read texts and other books with increasing independence. Yet, adjusting reading strategies when comprehension becomes difficult is a late-developing skill. Many college students fail to monitor their comprehension while reading (Glenberg and Epstein 1987). Instructing students in comprehension-

monitoring strategies in middle and high schools is imperative. Because good readers understand the goals of reading (Winograd 1984), it is important to articulate the purpose of individual reading assignments. Good readers also are able to use introductory and concluding sections to facilitate comprehension. One successful classroom strategy to build comprehension is to require students to paraphrase the first and last sections of an assignment before reading the rest of it.

Another characteristic of good readers that should be developed in middle and high school is the ability to vary reading rate according to level of difficulty. Teachers can help students understand how they vary their reading rate by having them estimate and write down how fast they read the newspaper, a science textbook, a mystery novel, and other material. Then they can work with the students on when they might want to skim, read rapidly, read at an average rate, and read slowly, depending on the information they want to retain from their reading. Teachers might also help students with the steps in the SQ4R technique first developed by Robinson in the 1940s, which teaches students to Survey, Question, Read and Reflect, Recite, and Review when reading.

Students need to learn how to analyze learning problems strategically. For example, a middle school teacher typically assigned fifteen vocabulary words that came from units the students were studying in history, science, and English. They were given the list on Monday and quizzed on Friday. To be effective and efficient learners, however, the students needed to be taught to analyze the list prior to study. For instance, they should know to divide the list into subject areas and eliminate known words and concentrate on the unknowns for further study. They should learn and apply organizational, elimination, and mnemonic strategies for the "odd words" in the list with unfamiliar spelling patterns.

Sometimes, the teacher can introduce an adjustment in a study technique that brings results. Students in one middle school teacher's class were consistently failing quizzes on vocabulary assigned from a literature-based reading program. The students needed to spell each word, give a brief definition, and use the word in a sentence. After several

weeks of exhorting the students to study from worksheets, the teacher tried a different approach. The students wrote each word on one side of an index card and the definition on the other. They wrote sentences using each word for homework. Then the teacher set aside 10 minutes of class time for the students to check each other's cards for accuracy and completeness. The day before the quiz, the teacher set aside 20 minutes for the students to quiz each other in small groups. Quiz grades shot up, and the students began recognizing the words in other contexts.

# CRITICAL THINKING AND PROBLEM SOLVING

Students need to learn problem-solving strategies across discipline areas. Middle and high school students understand the difference between problems that have open or heuristic solutions versus problems that have fixed or algorithmic solutions. The differentiation and solution of these two types of problems involve critical thinking skills, which cooperative group work often facilitates. Teachers can also introduce brainstorming sessions to foster critical thinking and problem solving. The brainstorming can focus on identifying and using some of the strategies described in this chapter. For example, the teacher can say, "The problem we have is that people do not seem to be organized. How can we go about solving it?" There is no one solution, but the students should be able to develop several likely heuristic solutions. They can also brainstorm to come up with algorithmic solutions, such as when they work on math problems in a small group.

# MONITORING LEARNING

Monitoring or self-regulating learning is perhaps the most critical skill that middle and high school students must develop to become independent learners. Scheduling and time management, increasing on-task and engaged time,

predicting quiz and test grades, and increasing comprehension awareness all have elements of self-regulation. Provision of evaluation rubrics to students also aids their self-assessment of products and leads to more accurate grade prediction. The development of monitoring skills goes hand in hand with the learner's growing awareness of an individual study style. Students must be involved in actively developing their own personal strategies for learning, problem solving, and remembering. Students must learn to develop strategies that work for *them.*

Teachers often want to increase classroom participation to engender active learning and to reinforce students' efforts to monitor the quantity and quality of their class involvement. A "classroom participation monitoring sheet," as shown in Figure 4.6, allows students to track themselves.

## FIGURE 4.6
### Classroom Participation Monitoring Sheet

Name: _____

Class:_____

Every time you raise your hand to answer a question, ask a question related to class material, or volunteer to put a problem on the board, mark it on the sheet. Keep the sheet on your desk in a convenient place. Try to improve your participation during the month.

| Date | Times I raised my hand to answer | Times I asked a relevant question | Times I volunteered to put a problem on the board |
|---|---|---|---|
|  |  |  |  |
|  |  |  |  |
|  |  |  |  |
|  |  |  |  |
|  |  |  |  |
|  |  |  |  |
|  |  |  |  |

# MAKING THE MOST OF STUDY SKILLS CLASSES

The study skills course, learning strategies lab, or reading skills class can serve as an advance organizer, although it cannot replace what is gained through embedded strategies to independent learning. Many detached courses or study skills labs attempt to teach skills by having students complete worksheets about organizational and listening skills, note taking, memory strategies, comprehension, and problem solving. Divorced from actual content, these exercises often are meaningless and irrelevant to students who fail to generalize the skills to their other courses.

Figure 4.7 shows a possible outline of topics that can be covered in a detached format along with examples of specific strategies to be taught. As they go through the topics, students apply the techniques they learn to their other courses. (For a review of the specific strategies included, see Rafoth, Leal, and DeFabo 1993.)

Another relevant and ultimately more successful approach with adolescents is to allow them to use the allotted time to discover "the skills of the good student" for themselves through a series of exercises. Johnson (in Branscombe, Goswami, and Schwartz 1990) recommends this approach in "In Search of the Good Student." To determine what a good student is and does and how he or she thinks and behaves, students are directed to look at family members, peers, teachers, coaches, and others around them. Students are given a single question to research, rather than a series of worksheets that they typically view as boring, busy work. The question—

What makes someone a good student?

This single question stimulates a good deal of initial class discussion. Students generate a number of different avenues to explore to answer the question. Surveys and interviews are a good experience for students. Interviews with parents, teachers, and coaches help students realize that adults who

# FIGURE 4.7
## Study Skills Course Outline

| WEEK AND TOPIC | SUGGESTED TECHNIQUES |
|---|---|
| **Week One**<br><br>Organizational Skills | • Effective listening (Message Game, questions for good listeners, following oral directions while listening)<br>• PREPARE Strategy<br>• SOLVER Strategy<br>• Using assignment books, schedules (Assignment Book Swap)<br><br>Lab Day—check student assignment books for use of strategies |
| **Week Two**<br><br>Reading Comprehension | • SQ4R/PQ4R<br>• Multipass Method<br>• Elaboration / "Look Back" Strategy<br>• Use of role play<br>• DISSECT (vocabulary)<br>• RAP (paragraph comprehension)<br><br>Lab Day—reading texts with one strategy |
| **Week Three**<br><br>Note-Taking Skills | • Concept-mapping<br>• Picking up cue words/actions<br>• Using abbreviations<br>• Modeling with overhead/Providing feedback<br>• Elaborating on notes<br>• Outlining/DNA Method/Cornell Method<br><br>Lab Day — taking notes, partner exchange feedback |
| **Week Four**<br><br>Monitoring Skills | • WRITER Strategy for language arts<br>• Estimation strategies (math, science)<br>• Self-testing strategies<br><br>Lab Day — practice self-testing, estimation, WRITER technique with partner, predicting (test grades) |

*—continued*

**Week Five**

Mnemonic
Skills

- Keyword Method
- Linking / Chain Mnemonics
- Rhymes
- Comparative Organizers
- "Wh" Questions
- First Letter Mnemonics
- Imagery
- Loci Method
- Chunking / Organization strategies
- CANDO Strategy

Lab Day — practice with problems from actual classes

**Week Six**

Critical
Thinking and
Problem-
Solving

- Means-End Analysis
- IDEAL Strategy
- "Talk It Through" Strategy
- SQRQCQ strategy (math)

Lab Day—practice with problems from actual classes

**Week Seven**

Preparation
and Test
Taking

- SCORER Strategy
- Monitoring and predicting
- Guidelines for preparing and taking tests
- Distributed study
- Analyzing incorrect answers

Lab Day—analyze own wrong answers/receive feedback—prepare study plan for upcoming test

**Week Eight**

Personal
Study Style
Development

- Retake Metacognitive and Study Skills Interviews—Present assignment book
- Example of notes with elaboration
- Test study plan
- Mnemonic examples
- Example of using SQ4R or other reading strategy with actual test
- Use strategy to solve problem
- Use monitoring strategy

are significant in their lives have been students themselves, and still are students who continue to learn on the job and in their private lives, reinforcing independent learning skills in a personally relevant way. Students' next task is to identify a list of attributes of the "good" student. They can then match their own skills and habits with the list to self-evaluate how far along they are on the road to becoming a "good" student.

## SUMMARY

Middle and high school teachers expect students to have mastered their own strategies for independent learning. As discussed in this chapter, this is often not the case. Students have the metacognitive ability to organize themselves, analyze problems, and monitor their work. However, without assistance from content and study skills teachers, they often cannot use these strategies on their own. Again, the role of the teacher in inspiring independent learning is critical.

# Assessment and Interventions

## CHAPTER 5

# Assessing Metacognitive and Study Skills

Often students who are having difficulty in the classroom do not have effective learning and study strategies. They may know about cognitive processes and how they work but have few strategies or fail to use their strategies in appropriate learning situations. In addition, some students are unable to monitor their learning, which is an essential part of developing independent learning skills.

To assess and design effective interventions for students in grades 3 and above, teachers, school psychologists, and other members of the school support team can use the Metacognitive Interview (Appendix A) and the Study Skills Interview (Appendix B). The Metacognitive Interview assesses students' overall awareness of how they learn and remember. The Study Skills Interview looks at how students perform their studying tasks in various subjects and focuses on the subject they find most difficult. Each interview takes about 20 to 30 minutes to administer. They can result in the creation of learner profiles and intervention programs for individual students or whole classes.

# THE TWO INTERVIEWS

The Metacognitive Interview was orignially developed by investigators at Tulane University who were examining teachers' expectations of their students' learning strategies. The current authors adapted the questionnaire for use with students and broadened the questions to encompass the areas of reading comprehension, note taking, and problem solving. A readability study found that the interview is written on a sixth-grade level. The interviewer typically reads the questions and possible responses out loud to avoid any confusion for students who may have reading difficulties.

The interview poses 25 questions or scenarios to students in three areas: metacognitive knowledge, metacognitive skills and strategies, and monitoring and self-awareness. In the first two sections, students listen to different learning scenarios and then answer questions. For example, in the knowledge section, students predict how many numbers in a sequence they might accurately remember. In the skills and strategies section, students say what they would do in a particular study or learning scenario, such as when they must read to prepare for a quiz. In the monitoring and self-awareness section, students respond to true-false questions that elicit information about how confident and aware they are of their own learning. For example, students are asked if they can predict what score they will receive on a test and if they know whether or not they have answered an individual question correctly.

With the results of the interview, a Student Profile can be prepared for an individual child or a class. The profile includes 20 descriptors representative of the three areas of the interview (Figure 5.1), and students are rated with a "Yes," "No," or "Emerging" in each. An Intervention Plan can focus on the areas in which the student has no or only an emerging level of mastery.

The Study Skills Interview (Appendix B) more informally measures how students respond to their current school tasks. Students describe how they are tested and how they prepare both in and out of class in major content areas, how they schedule their study and review time, and how

they study for their most difficult subject. The person administering the interview completes a subjective profile of the student. For each subject area, the student's current study strategies are rated on a continuum from 1 to 5, or inefficient to efficient. The profile lists a menu of potential remedial strategies. The teacher recommends specific strategies by underlining or circling those that she or he feels can best benefit the student.

By using the Metacognitive Interview and the Study Skills Interview together, a teacher can produce a picture of a student's metacognitive sophistication and the effectiveness of his or her current study practices. As shown in the three case studies below, such informal assessments and student profiles have led to effective classroom interventions by individual teachers, child study teams, and instructional support teams in schools.

# WORKING WITH INDIVIDUAL STUDENTS

The following case studies show how the interviews were used to profile and suggest tailored learning strategies for three students—a third grader, a seventh grader, and a twelfth grader. These profiles also illustrate the gradual and steady acquisition of metacognitive knowledge and skills as children mature. Thus, the high school student has much higher metacognitive skills than the seventh grader, who in turn is stronger metacognitively than the third grader. However, each of the students had specific weaknesses that could be remediated to increase academic achievement and independent learning skills.

## *Jake: A Bright Third Grader with Attention Problems*

**ASSESSMENT.** Jake is a nine-year-old in the third grade. His Metacognitive Interview Profile (Figure 5.2) shows that he understands interference, or how new information can "interfere" in his mind with already acquired information. He knows that it is easier to remember the gist of something than to recall it verbatim, but he has some uncertainty about the limits of his short-term memory and the ways

## FIGURE 5.1
### Metacognitive Interview Categories

| Metacognitive Knowledge | Metacognitive Skills and Strategies | Monitoring and Self-Awareness |
|---|---|---|
| Understands interference | Paraphrases information to aid recall in reading comprehension | Varies study to meet task demands |
| Knows limits of short-term memory | Uses repetition to aid comprehension and memory | Divides study time effectively |
| Knows effective aids to memorization | Uses notes as external aids for recall | Has a sense of metacognitive awareness |
| Understands recall of meaningful material | Uses rehearsal effectively | Predicts exam grades successfully |
| Understands that meaning increases ease of rote memory | Uses categorization/ chunking strategies | Directs self to perform learning strategies |
| Understands that preview increases comprehension | Self-tests while studying | Senses poor comprehension and reviews material |
| Understands that directing attention to key information increases retention | | Uses estimation/ prediction to monitor performance |

to remember information. His interview revealed that he does not understand that meaningfulness increases the ease of memory, does not know to preview a text before reading it, and does not realize that directing attention to key information (as in highlighting) helps memory. These weaknesses are to be expected in a child his age. Although, his indication that he uses notes is somewhat unusual for a child his age. Jake does not put information into his own words while reading, although he does know to rehearse

and read something repeatedly to increase retention. Jake does not use rehearsal effectively—meaning that when Jake rehearses something, he does not do it in the same way that he will have to recall it. He does not know to group or chunk information and is only beginning to self-test.

Jake's monitoring skills appear to be fairly mature. He indicates that he does different things when he studies for different types of tasks and studies harder topics for a longer amount of time than easier topics. He is somewhat able to predict test grades and indicates that he instructs himself to perform learning strategies. He does not always sense when he does not understand something while reading, however. It is interesting to note that he uses estimation or prediction to monitor performance. This may be related to the emphasis his math curriculum places on estimation.

In school, Jake is a bright student, but has been identified with attention problems. This is evident on Jake's Study Skills Interview Profile (Figure 5.3). He says that he uses visual imagery to help himself organize material, but also indicates that he does not effectively or diligently rehearse information that he has to recall. He appears to be fairly flexible in his ability to use time effectively. For example, his mother encourages him to study while they are driving in the car and tests him with flash cards. Another positive note is Jake's knowledge of when tests will occur and what kind of tests will be given. Yet, Jake appeared to contradict himself when discussing social studies, his hardest subject. Once he said that he had a test every two weeks, and then later in the interview, he said he did not know when he was tested. He also does not indicate distributed study, but rather studies the night before a test. Overall, Jake presents good metacognitive and study skills development for a student his age. However, he uses many inefficient techniques.

**INTERVENTIONS.** Recommendations for Jake include studying for spelling with an initial self-test to eliminate known words. (This and other recommendations are underlined on his Study Skills Interview Profile in Figure 5.3.) He could then analyze unknown words before creating the visual images he uses in his head to help remember them.

# FIGURE 5.2*
## Jake's Metacognitive Interview Profile

Student Name: __Jake__     Grade: __3__     Age: __9__

| Metacognitive Knowledge: | Yes | Emerging | No |
|---|---|---|---|
| 1. Understands interference | X | | |
| 2. Knows limits of short-term memory | | X | |
| 3. Knows effective aids to memorization | | X | |
| 4. Understands recall or meaningful material (gist vs. verbatim) | | X | |
| 5. Understands that meaning increases ease of rote memory | | | X |
| 6. Understands that preview increases comprehension | | | X |
| 7. Understands that directing attention to key information increases retention | | | X |

| Metacognitive Skills and Strategies: | Yes | Emerging | No |
|---|---|---|---|
| 8. Paraphrases information to aid recall in reading comprehension | | | X |
| 9. Uses repetition to aid comprehension and memory | X | | |
| 10. Uses notes as external aids for recall | X | | |
| 11. Uses rehearsal effectively | | X | |
| 12. Uses categorization/chunking strategies | | | X |
| 13. Self-tests while studying | | X | |

| Monitoring and Self-Awareness: | Yes | Emerging | No |
|---|---|---|---|
| 14. Varies study techniques to meet task demands | X | | |
| 15. Divides study time effectively | | | X |
| 16. Has a sense of metacognitive awareness (knowing you know) | | X | |
| 17. Predicts exam grades successfully | | X | |
| 18. Directs self to perform learning strategies | X | | |
| 19. Senses poor comprehension and reviews material | | X | |
| 20. Uses estimation/prediction to monitor performance | X | | |

*A blank Metacognitive Interview Profile appears in Appendix A.

# FIGURE 5.3*
## Jake's Study Skills Interview Profile

Student Name: __Jake__    Grade: __3__    Age: __9__

Strategy Use

| Subject Area | Inefficient Efficient | Recommendation |
|---|---|---|
| Spelling | _____<br>1 2 **3** 4 5 | Self-test initially; eliminate knowns; analyze unknown; rehearse/mnemonics; paired associate task; self-test |
| History/<br>Social Studies | _____<br>1 2 **3** 4 5 | Incorporate SQ4R; make summary during "recite/reflect" phase; apply mnemonics to information on worksheets; review studying for and taking multiple choice, true-false, fill-ins |
| Science | _____<br>1 2 3 **4** 5 | Incorporate SQ4R; note-taking strategies; studying fill-ins, multiple choice, true-false |
| Math | _____<br>1 2 **3** 4 5 | Work new practice problems and check; estimation strategies to check work |
| Hardest Subject | _____<br>1 2 **3** 4 5 | SQ4R; increase strategies for increasing text comprehension; test-taking strategies; mnemonics; note-taking skills |
| Distributed Study | _____<br>**1** 2 3 4 5 | Prior to test review several nights; make study cards that can be reviewed throughout the day |

*A blank Study Skills Interview Profile appears in Appendix B.

He also is unsure about effective reading comprehension techniques. Given Jake's attention difficulties, it would be effective to work through a specific method of increasing text comprehension. For example, he might use a simplification of the SQ4R technique, in which he skims or looks through a chapter before reading it, writes down one or two key questions he thinks will be answered in the chapter, and actively paraphrases information during and after reading the text. Jake also indicates that he often studies from worksheets or study sheets. He should be encouraged to apply mnemonics in chunking strategies to help him recall information. In math, Jake said that the only thing he studied was information that required rote memorization skills such as the multiplication tables. He needs to learn to work new practice problems and to check himself through estimation strategies as he enters the upper grades.

Jake did not make any differentiation between how he studied and the kind of test he is given, so discussions of how to study for different kinds of tests are also appropriate. Because Jake already studies during the day when he has extra time, he should use more flash cards. In fact, studying in short bursts is particularly effective for a child with attentional difficulties.

Finally, because Jake appears to have good monitoring skills for a student his age, he should use these skills to help him monitor his own attention in the classroom. Strategies to monitor his attention might include having him mark on a little card taped to his desk whether or not he had been paying attention at different intervals during the day. He could then compare points at which he felt he was paying attention with his success in the classroom. Even if Jake is not accurate in his evaluation of when he is attentive and when he is not, his overall attention should improve. Research indicates that when students monitor themselves, overall attention and productivity increase even when they are inaccurate in their judgments (Halihan et al. 1983).

## Kitty: A Seventh Grader with Inefficient Study Skills

**ASSESSMENT.** Kitty is a seventh grader having difficulty in her English and world culture classes. Her metacognitive

# FIGURE 5.4
## Kitty's Metacognitive Interview Profile

Student Name: __Kitty__    Grade: __7__    Age: __13__

| Metacognitive Knowledge: | Yes | Emerging | No |
|---|---|---|---|
| 1. Understands interference | | X | |
| 2. Knows limits of short-term memory | X | | |
| 3. Knows effective aids to memorization | | | X |
| 4. Understands recall or meaningful material (gist vs. verbatim) | | X | |
| 5. Understands that meaning increases ease of rote memory | | | X |
| 6. Understands that preview increases comprehension | | X | |
| 7. Understands that directing attention to key information increases retention | | | X |

| Metacognitive Skills and Strategies: | | | |
|---|---|---|---|
| 8. Paraphrases information to aid recall in reading comprehension | X | | |
| 9. Uses repetition to aid comprehension and memory | X | | |
| 10. Uses notes as external aids for recall | | X | |
| 11. Uses rehearsal effectively | X | | |
| 12. Uses categorization/chunking strategies | | X | |
| 13. Self-tests while studying | X | | |

| Monitoring and Self-Awareness: | | | |
|---|---|---|---|
| 14. Varies study techniques to meet task demands | X | | |
| 15. Divides study time effectively | X | | |
| 16. Has a sense of metacognitive awareness (knowing you know) | X | | |
| 17. Predicts exam grades successfully | | | X |
| 18. Directs self to perform learning strategies | X | | |
| 19. Senses poor comprehension and reviews material | X | | |
| 20. Uses estimation/prediction to monitor performance | | X | |

knowledge is fairly good (Figure 5.4). However, she only understands the concept of interference in an imperfect way and does not understand that meaningfulness increases the ease of rote memory. She does not know that previewing would aid her comprehension or increase the limits of her short-term memory. She cannot highlight text effectively or draw on effective aids to memorization. She seems to have good metacognitive strategies, indicating that she knows how to paraphrase information, use repetition rehearsal effectively, and self-test. However, she is only beginning to use notes to aid recall and does not use effective categorization strategies in studying.

While Kitty's monitoring skills appear to be good overall, she is unable to predict her exam grades and only occasionally uses estimation to predict and monitor performance.

Kitty's Study Skills Interview Profile indicates her overdependence on rehearsal and repetition as strategies (Figure 5.5). For example, to study vocabulary words, she said that she writes each word five times and then asks her parent to quiz her. She repeats the words she gets wrong seven times; again Kitty uses a "magic number" of repetitions as her main means of studying rather than a self-test. Although her teachers and parents have given her more effective strategies like acrostics to help remember information, repetition remains her main approach. Kitty's rehearsal strategies lead to a fairly effective approach to math, however. She said that she takes two problems from each section in her math text and does five problems for every problem that she gets wrong. While Kitty's approach ensures enough rehearsal, it lacks efficiency. For example, if she were to self-test initially, she might not need to do problems from all sections and could concentrate all of her time on those problems of which she is unsure. She identified her hardest subject as world cultures, a subject in which she had a D at mid-point but raised to a B by completing extra-credit work. Again, here she does not indicate very efficient study strategies. She writes down the key words the teacher puts on the board and just "tries to remember them." Also, she indicates that the teacher does not do much distributed testing in that class. Kitty said she only had "one big test so far."

**INTERVENTIONS.** Kitty would benefit from more frequent

## FIGURE 5.5
### Kitty's Study Skills Interview Profile

Student Name: __Kitty__     Grade: __7__     Age: __13__

| Subject Area | Strategy Use Inefficient Efficient | Recommendation |
|---|---|---|
| Spelling | 1 <u>2</u> 3 4 5 | Self-test initially; eliminate knowns; analyze unknown; rehearse/mnemonics; paired associate task; self-test |
| History/ Social Studies | 1 <u>2</u> 3 4 5 | Incorporate SQ4R; make summary during "recite/ reflect" phase; apply mnemonics to information on worksheets; review studying for and taking multiple choice, true/false, fill-ins |
| Science | 1 2 <u>3</u> 4 5 | Incorporate SQ4R; note-taking strategies; study-ing fill-ins, multiple choice, true/false |
| Math | 1 2 3 <u>4</u> 5 | Work new practice prob-lems and check, estima-ation strategies to check work |
| Hardest Subject | 1 <u>2</u> 3 4 5 | SQ4R; increase strategies for increasing text compre-hension; test-taking strate gies; mnemonics; note-taking skills |
| Distributed Study | 1 2 3 <u>4</u> 5 | Prior to test review several nights; make study cards that can be reviewed throughout the day |

testing. She indicated that she tries to study a week in advance and to study a little bit each night for a test but acknowledges that this is sometimes not possible because of her other homework. If she did more self-testing, she could

concentrate on what she still does not know, instead of trying to cover everything in the same amount. She needs to get away from relying on the "magic number" of repetition. She wants to succeed. Overall, her metacognitive study skills are good, although she shows an overdependence on rehearsal and rote strategies. Kitty needs to learn how to study material in a distributed fashion and how to effectively use mnemonics and paraphrasing as strategies to help make material more meaningful to her. She should also make study cards, which she could use when she has a few minutes during the day.

## *Jim: Twelfth Grader Still Relying on Repetition*

**ASSESSMENT.** As might be expected for a twelfth grader, Jim answered all of the questions assessing knowledge and skills correctly in the Metacognitive Interview Profile (Figure 5.6). He also indicated good monitoring and self-awareness skills, receiving an emerging score only in the ability to direct himself to perform specific kinds of strategies for different kinds of learning tasks. In fact, this would appear to be Jim's main weakness.

Jim's Study Skills Interview Profile (Figure 5.7) indicates that his basic approach to studying is still repetition. He said that he studies for vocabulary tests by copying the letters over and over and then saying them "over and over" in his head. In social studies he goes over his notes "over and over again" until "I can remember them in my head." Similarly, in math he copies examples from the board and goes over the same ones in order to understand them. This is probably why calculus is his hardest course. He receives scores in the C range even though his other grades are typically higher.

**INTERVENTIONS.** Jim needs more effective study techniques, particularly for mathematics. He needs to identify the kinds of problems that are going to be on a test and review examples in class, as well as work new practice problems in order to assure comprehension.

He also needs to study every night. He indicated that he only studies the night before a test. By grade twelve, students should be using more distributed study practices,

# FIGURE 5.6
## Jim's Metacognitive Interview Profile

Student Name: __Jim__    Grade: __12__    Age: __17__

| Metacognitive Knowledge: | Yes | Emerging | No |
|---|:---:|:---:|:---:|
| 1. Understands interference | X | | |
| 2. Knows limits of short-term memory | X | | |
| 3. Knows effective aids to memorization | X | | |
| 4. Understands recall or meaningful material (gist vs. verbatim) | X | | |
| 5. Understands that meaning increases ease of rote memory | X | | |
| 6. Understands that preview increases comprehension | X | | |
| 7. Understands that directing attention to key information increases retention | X | | |

| Metacognitive Skills and Strategies: | | | |
|---|:---:|:---:|:---:|
| 8. Paraphrases information to aid recall in reading comprehension | X | | |
| 9. Uses repetition to aid comprehension and memory | X | | |
| 10. Uses notes as external aids for recall | X | | |
| 11. Uses rehearsal effectively | X | | |
| 12. Uses categorization/chunking strategies | X | | |
| 13. Self-tests while studying | X | | |

| Monitoring and Self-Awareness: | | | |
|---|:---:|:---:|:---:|
| 14. Varies study techniques to meet task demands | X | | |
| 15. Divides study time effectively | X | | |
| 16. Has a sense of metacognitive awareness (knowing you know) | X | | |
| 17. Predicts exam grades successfully | X | | |
| 18. Directs self to perform learning strategies | | X | |
| 19. Senses poor comprehension and reviews material | X | | |
| 20. Uses estimation/prediction to monitor performance | X | | |

which they will need in college. Elementary school teachers assess children frequently and daily samples of work and weekly quizzes are common. As children get older, however, evaluation becomes less frequent, often limited to two or three major tests per semester. This is particularly true at the college level. Thus, for true independent learning to develop, students must learn to enforce distributed learning on their own and to study and quiz themselves on a daily and weekly basis.

## FIGURE 5.7
### Jim's Study Skills Interview Profile

Student Name: _Jim_    Grade: _12_    Age: _17_

Strategy Use

| Subject Area | Inefficient Efficient | Recommendation |
|---|---|---|
| Spelling | _____<br>1 2 **3** 4 5 | Self-test initially; eliminate knowns; analyze unknown; rehearse/mnemonics; paired associate task; self-test |
| History/ Social Studies | _____<br>1 2 **3** 4 5 | Incorporate SQ4R; make summary during "recite/ reflect" phase; apply mnemonics to information on worksheets; review studying for and taking multiple choice, true/false, fill-ins |
| Science | _____<br>1 2 **3** 4 5 | Incorporate SQ4R; note-taking strategies; studing fill-ins, imultiple choice, true/ false |
| Math | _____<br>1 **2** 3 4 5 | Work new practice problems and check; esitmation strategies to check work |
| Hardest Subject | _____<br>1 **2** 3 4 5 | SQ4R; increase strategies for increasing text comprehension; test-taking strategies; mnemonics; note-taking skill |
| Distributed Study | _____<br>**1** 2 3 4 5 | Prior to test review several nights; make study cards that can be reviewed throughout the day |

# WORKING WITH AN ENTIRE CLASS

**ASSESSMENT.** The Metacognitive and Study Skills Interviews can also be used for a whole classroom. Figure 5.8 shows student profile results of the Metacognitive Interview for a class of seventh graders identified by their district as a "low math group." Their teacher was concerned that the students did not have good study skills or strong awareness of their own learning and wanted some direction in how to intervene. The class took the Metacognitive Interview together. The teacher read the questions and answers out loud, and then compiled the results. As can be seen in Figure 5.8, a majority of the students in the class did not know effective aids to memorization, did not understand that preview increased comprehension, and did not know the purpose of highlighting a text or worksheet.

In addition, three-fourths of the students in the class did not use categorization or chunking strategies and a small, but significant number (17 percent) did not self-test while studying or even use repetition to aid comprehension and memory. A majority of the class did not use notes as external aids for recall. Perhaps most striking, only 8 percent of the students in this class could predict their exam grades successfully, and none of them sensed poor comprehension when they read or spontaneously reviewed material. Only a minority of the class used estimation to check their work or monitor their performance.

A fourth of the class had no sense of metacognitive awareness; in other words, they never had the feeling that they knew something but were just not able to recall it. A small but significant number did not vary their study techniques to meet task demands or direct themselves to perform learning strategies.

**INTERVENTIONS.** To come up with intervention techniques for this class, the teacher targeted the areas of weakness identified through the assessment. Initially, the teacher completed some in-class exercises to help students learn about memory and comprehension. Because many of the students indicated that they did not understand that

# FIGURE 5.8
## Metacognitive Interview Profile

Student Profile – 7th Grade "Low" Math Class

| Metacognitive Knowledge: | Yes (%) | Emerging (%) | No (%) |
|---|---|---|---|
| 1. Understands interference | 83 | | 17 |
| 2. Knows limits of short-term memory | 66 | 17 | 17 |
| 3. Knows effective aids to memorization | 25 | 66 | 8 |
| 4. Understands recall or meaningful material (gist vs. verbatim) | 83 | | 17 |
| 5. Understands that meaning increases ease of rote memory | 92 | | 8 |
| 6. Understands that preview increases comprehension | 42 | | 58 |
| 7. Understands that directing attention to key information increases retention | 50 | | 50 |
| **Metacognitive Skills and Strategies:** | | | |
| 8. Paraphrases information to aid recall in reading comprehension | 66 | | 34 |
| 9. Uses repetition to aid comprehension and memory | 83 | | 17 |
| 10. Uses notes as external aids for recall | 25 | 58 | 17 |
| 11. Uses rehearsal effectively | 58 | 25 | 17 |
| 12. Uses categorization/chunking strategies | 25 | | 75 |
| 13. Self-tests while studying | 83 | | 17 |
| **Monitoring and Self-Awareness:** | 83 | | 17 |
| 14. Varies study techniques to meet task demands | 83 | | 17 |
| 15. Divides study time effectively | 58 | 34 | 8 |
| 16. Has a sense of metacognitive awareness (knowing you know) | 75 | | 25 |
| 17. Predicts exam grades successfully | 8 | 25 | 67 |
| 18. Directs self to perform learning strategies | 34 | 58 | 8 |
| 19. Senses poor comprehension and reviews material | 83 | | 17 |
| 20. Uses estimation/prediction to monitor performance | 33 | 50 | 17 |

preview aided comprehension, the teacher demonstrated previewing by using their math text. Similarly, because many of the students in the class (50 percent) did not understand the purpose of highlighting, the teacher copied math worksheets that allowed the students to use highlighters to direct and focus their attention and to aid recall. Because many students did not know effective aids to memorization, the teacher introduced mnemonic aids and applied them to important mathematical formulas and definitions. Finally, the students reviewed the seven areas covered in the knowledge section of the Metacognitive Interview.

In order to remediate some of the students' skills and strategies deficits, the teacher targeted two key areas: using notes as external aids to recall and using categorization and chunking strategies. The teacher reviewed her expectations of note taking, worked with a consultant to make her lessons easier to take notes from, and adapted a system of note taking in mathematics proven to work. (See Chapter 4, Figure 4.4.)

In addition, the teacher modeled chunking and categorization strategies to show students how they would find it easier to remember mathematical terms and definitions and formulas by grouping or chunking the information. She used a combination approach of chunking and note taking by having the students go through their notebooks with a highlighter. They learned to block off and group different sections so that when they studied, they could separate one topic from another. Because some students indicated they did not have skills in each of the six areas covered in the skills and strategies section of the Metacognitive Interview, she reviewed these areas.

Finally, many students indicated that they could not predict their exam grades. To intervene in this area, the teacher developed a chart of daily predictions. Students marked on the chart whether or not they had understood the class material, whether they needed review that day, and what they estimated their grade would be on weekly quizzes. Students who estimated their grade accurately received two bonus points. Students also estimated their test grades and received five bonus points for an accurate

estimate. They completed self-tests prior to their unit test in order to help them evaluate what their performance would be on the real test. Estimation strategies were also emphasized in their daily work to help them connect estimation and self-checking with monitoring of comprehension.

# SUMMARY

Students display a great deal of variability in the kinds of metacognitive knowledge they have, the types of strategies they use, and their self-awareness regarding their own learning and remembering. The Metacognitive and Study Skills Interviews are two tools to help in the assessment of students' strengths and weaknesses. Informal assessment of students' metacognitive knowledge and skills and their current study practices can lead to effective, individualized intervention. Instructional support and child study teams can use both the Metacognitive Intervention Form in Appendix A and the Study Skills Profile in Appendix B to develop individualized plans for students having difficulty in the classroom. Such plans are particularly helpful for students who may be inclusioned into regular classrooms or who are being mainstreamed into regular classrooms from self-contained programs.

# CHAPTER 6

# Peer Tutoring and Independent Learning

Peer tutoring is an effective means to increase academic achievement and benefits both the tutor and the target student (sometimes called the tutee). This chapter describes a model that combines the traditional use of a peer tutor (content-area instructional aid) with a complementary use (study skills or learning strategies coach). Research has shown that the knowledge of study skills, acquisition of learning strategies, and their successful application in the classroom separate children who achieve from children who do not to a greater extent than does ability or IQ (Morris 1990; Swanson 1990). Successful students know how to study, prepare for exams, identify important information in teacher "talk," and monitor their own learning. In using peer tutors as study skills coaches, this model emphasizes the tutors' need to "share the secret" of successful learning with their target students.

In peer-tutoring programs, academic achievement and self-esteem can increase for both the tutor and the tutee. In the Share the Secret Program described in this chapter, other benefits also accrued. Target students learned *how* to study and received specific help on content. Both the tutors and tutees increased awareness of their current study and learning strategies. The tutors improved their effectiveness

as tutors from a traditional content perspective and also learned to analyze and share the secret of their academic success.

The Share the Secret Program trained tutors to intervene with high-risk students who were underachieving in school and considered likely to drop out. The tutors received training in learning strategies and study skills, focusing on how to embed the strategies into specific content areas. After the training, an average tutor worked individually with four students for about 15 to 30 minutes each, two to four times a week, usually during study hall. They mostly helped with homework, but also explained content covered in the students' classes and different study methods.

## INCREASING STUDENT AWARENESS OF METACOGNITIVE AND STUDY SKILLS

Students chosen to work as tutors were already members of a peer-helping club at their school. They were good students academically and were judged to have the maturity to work with peers. Students targeted as tutees were having academic difficulty as ninth and tenth graders. They did not have high absenteeism or major discipline problems. Thus, it was logical to conclude that many of their academic problems stemmed from poor study and learning skills.

As the first step in the program, both the tutors and the tutees took the Metacognitive Interview discussed in Chapter 5. The tutors showed overwhelmingly stronger strategic learning skills. They had strong knowledge of memory and comprehension strategies, tended to use these strategies, and had a good sense of their own learning relative to their ability to monitor themselves.

In contrast, most of the students targeted to be tutored had weak knowledge of memory and comprehension strategies, tended not to use these strategies, and were not strong with regard to their ability to monitor their learning.

The performances of the tutors on the Metacognitive Interview and the performance of the students chosen to receive tutoring are compared in Figures 6.1 and 6.2 (Rafoth 1996).

# FIGURE 6.1
## Metacognitive Interview
## Student Profile—Peer Tutors

| Metacognitive Knowledge: | Yes (%) | Emerging (%) | No (%) |
|---|---|---|---|
| 1. Understands interference | 74 | | 26 |
| 2. Knows limits of short-term memory | 70 | 30 | |
| 3. Knows effective aids to memorization | 57 | 43 | |
| 4. Understands recall of meaningful material (gist vs. verbatim) | 94 | | 6 |
| 5. Understands that meaning increases ease of rote memory | 94 | | 6 |
| 6. Understands that preview increases comprehension | 91 | | 9 |
| 7. Understands that directing attention to key information increases retention | 94 | | 6 |
| **Metacognitive Skills and Strategies:** | | | |
| 8. Paraphrases information to aid recall in reading comprehension | 91 | | 9 |
| 9. Uses repetition to aid comprehension and memory | 94 | | 6 |
| 10. Uses notes as external aids for recall | 77 | 23 | |
| 11. Uses rehearsal effectively | 91 | 3 | 6 |
| 12. Uses categorization/chunking strategies | 69 | 14 | 17 |
| 13. Self-tests while studying | 94 | 3 | 3 |
| **Monitoring and Self-Awareness:** | | | |
| 14. Varies study techniques to meet task demands | 97 | | 3 |
| 15. Divides study time effectively | 86 | 14 | |
| 16. Has a sense of metacognitive awareness (knowing you know) | 91 | 9 | |
| 17. Predicts exam grades successfully | 83 | 14 | 3 |
| 18. Directs self to perform learning strategies | 77 | 20 | 3 |
| 19. Senses poor comprehension and reviews material | 69 | 31 | |
| 20. Uses estimation/prediction to monitor performance | 40 | 57 | 3 |

# Figure 6.2
## Metacognitive Interview
## Student Profile—At-Risk Students

| Metacognitive Knowledge: | Yes (%) | Emerging (%) | No (%) |
|---|---|---|---|
| 1. Understands interference | 40 | 10 | 50 |
| 2. Knows limits of short-term memory | 50 | 40 | 10 |
| 3. Knows effective aids to memorization | 35 | 50 | 15 |
| 4. Understands recall of meaningful material (gist vs. verbatim) | 85 | 5 | 10 |
| 5. Understands that meaning increases ease of rote memory | 85 | 10 | 5 |
| 6. Understands that preview increases comprehension | 55 | 5 | 40 |
| 7. Understands that directing attention to key information increases retention | 70 | 5 | 25 |
| **Metacognitive Skills and Strategies:** | | | |
| 8. Paraphrases information to aid recall in reading comprehension | 65 | | 35 |
| 9. Uses repetition to aid comprehension and memory | 75 | | 25 |
| 10. Uses notes as external aids for recall | 20 | 70 | 10 |
| 11. Uses rehearsal effectively | 45 | 25 | 30 |
| 12. Uses categorization/chunking strategies | 40 | 15 | 45 |
| 13. Self-tests while studying | 65 | 15 | 20 |
| **Monitoring and Self-awareness:** | | | |
| 14. Varies study techniques to meet task demands | 80 | | 20 |
| 15. Divides study time effectively | 55 | 40 | 5 |
| 16. Has a sense of metacognitive awareness (knowing you know) | 70 | 25 | 5 |
| 17. Predicts exam grades successfully | 60 | 10 | 30 |
| 18. Directs self to perform learning strategies | 35 | 55 | 10 |
| 19. Senses poor comprehension and reviews material | 20 | 55 | 25 |
| 20. Uses estimation/prediction to monitor performance | 25 | 45 | 30 |

# TRAINING THE TUTORS

The tutors participated in four training sessions. Many of the materials used in the sessions and as follow-up reference appear in a Peer Tutoring Manual, which is reprinted as Appendix C.

The tutors used their first two training sessions to review the results of the Metacognitive Interviews. They discussed the importance to effective learning of memory and comprehension strategies, note taking, and preparation for tests and exams. This procedure served to increase their knowledge and awareness of the strategies they used and helped them contrast their skills with the students they would be tutoring. A Student Profile, as described in Chapter 5, was prepared for each of the targeted students and shared with their tutors.

In these first two sessions, the tutors also learned how to discuss weak metacognitive areas, remediate areas in study skills, and prepare their tutees for tests (Rafoth, Leal, and DeFabo 1993). They reviewed prompts to use in the remediation or discussion of the performance of their tutees on the Metacognitive Interview. For example, if the tutee did not understand interference, the tutor was prompted to explain the concept of interference with the specific example of how to study for two tests scheduled for the same day.

In the third and fourth training sessions, the tutors developed more effective one-on-one tutoring skills. As a group, they weighed 15 different behaviors that lead to effective tutoring from the most to least important. They discussed principles through which students learn best, the characteristics of a successful tutor, and their responsibilities as a tutor (Sabrinsky 1992), all of which they could refer to in the Peer Tutoring Manual. They also discussed how they could help their tutees develop a rationale for school improvement and could serve as role models to the students they tutored. They were taught to encourage tutees by helping them arrive at the right answer, not telling them the answer. Tutors were encouraged to help their tutees realize *what* they had learned and to increase their awareness of

being in control of their own learning. Similarly, tutors learned how to help tutees understand what they still needed to learn and what material required further study.

The Peer Tutoring Manual included a form to help tutors prepare for their first meetings with the tutees. During these training sessions, tutors completed the forms individually and then discussed them in the large group. On the form, they said why they wanted to tutor, what they wanted to know about their tutee, and what they wanted to say to their tutees during their first meetings.

They also reviewed the importance of such interpersonal techniques as active listening, becoming familiar with the tutee's problem course, respecting the confidentiality of the sessions, and giving the tutee undivided attention during a tutoring session. Tutors learned how to keep a log of their activities after each tutoring session. The supervising teacher reviewed the logs biweekly. Tutors were also encouraged to ask for help when they needed it by going to either the supervising teacher or the tutees' teachers. Tutors were advised never to criticize teachers in the school or to criticize the type of instruction occurring in the class in which the tutee was having difficulty.

As a concluding training activity, students performed three exercises. In the first, small groups evaluated a series of comments and judged whether an effective tutor would make these comments. In the second, they looked at a series of comments that a tutee might make and considered what an effective tutor might say in response. The tutors participated in the third exercise after several tutoring sessions had taken place. In this exercise, the tutors did a self-evaluation to check whether or not they engaged in a series of proactive activities. This led to another discussion of appropriate and inappropriate activities during the tutoring sessions and allowed for group trouble-shooting.

# ENCOURAGING TUTORS TO BE STUDY SKILLS COACHES

Students who were chosen to be tutors acted as study skills coaches to their tutees. After seeing the difference between

their own approach to studying and that of their tutees in the Metacognitive Interviews, students learned how to help their tutees through completion of a Strategic Study Sheet (included in the Peer Tutoring Manual in Appendix C). On the sheet, tutors and tutees list the tutees' classes and summarize their current grades in quizzes, lab work, homework, exams, and other work. The students then brainstorm strategies to improve weak areas. For example, if the tutee is weak in lab work, the tutor and the tutee might brainstorm ways to work more effectively with a lab partner and review lab notes. If exams are the problem, the tutee and the tutor might emphasize preparing a study plan for a large exam or test. Finally, the tutor and tutee chart the progress made in each class as a result of the tutoring and agree upon rewards if the tutee meets a goal. The reward could be something that the tutee gives him or herself. For example, the tutee might write "if I make a C on this upcoming test, I will be allowed to see a movie with a friend." Or the tutor and the tutee might agree that they will spend five minutes in a conversation or a game if the tutee's grades improve to a certain level.

Tutors reviewed strategies for preparing for and taking tests and were encouraged to share this information, as well as mnemonic, note-taking, and other strategies, with their tutees. They were instructed to overtly explain how they talk themselves through problems and use different strategies to problem solve. Many of the strategies that the tutors learned to identify and discuss are explained throughout this book.

# RESULTS OF THE PROGRAM

A survey of the peer tutors and an open-ended interview with the tutees were used to evaluate the program. Other informative evaluation methods might include a comparison of pre- and post-program GPAs, attendance and disciplinary referral rates for students in the program compared with matched groups not in the program, and observations of tutoring sessions.

In the interviews, many students who had been tutored

said that they felt that their tutors "knew everything that they needed to know," "were able to push you to do the work because they did not want you to fail," "could explain something better to them than teachers," and provided them with some one-on-one attention (Rafoth 1996). Many indicated that sometimes they had difficulty asking teachers questions and felt they did not have access to teachers. However, they found the peer tutors accessible and easy to talk with. When asked to name one thing that they learned from the tutor, students indicated they learned specific strategies, such as different ways to remember spelling words; how to study and approach studying; the importance of applying effort and working consistently on homework and quizzes; and how to cooperate with other people (Rafoth 1996). Many also indicated that they earned better grades, got into less trouble in school (particularly in study hall), stayed on task and kept up with their homework better, and felt the effect of positive peer pressure to complete their homework and other class assignments (Rafoth 1996).

Results from one Share the Secret pilot program appear in Figure 6.3 (Rafoth 1996). The responses from the students indicate that both the tutors and the tutees felt that the tutees benefited and, in addition, most tutors rated it as a positive experience.

## SUMMARY

Adding a study skills coach component to a peer-tutoring program at the middle or high school level appears to be effective. Many of the students who received tutoring at the middle and high school levels in the Share the Secret Program significantly improved their grades and developed study skills they could apply to other learning situations. The Share the Secret Program, which stresses adequate tutor training, is a model that can be adapted to fit other tutoring situations.

# FIGURE 6.3
## Evaluation of Peer-Tutoring Program by Students

**Did Working With the Peer Tutor:**

| | Strongly Agree (%) | Agree (%) | No Opinion (%) | Disagree (%) | Strongly Disagree (%) |
|---|---|---|---|---|---|
| 1. Help you understand your work? | 100 | | | | |
| 2. Help you get your work done? | 100 | | | | |
| 3. Help improve grades on tests? | 100 | | | | |
| 4. Help improve your overall grade? | 100 | | | | |
| 5. Help you feel better about school? | 100 | | | | |
| 6. Help you learn how to study? | 94 | | 6 | | |
| 7. Help you study for tests? | 94 | | 6 | | |
| 8. Help you with homework? | 100 | | | | |
| 9. Do you consider the tutor a friend? | 88 | | 6 | 6 | |

**Evaluation of Peer Tutor Program by Tutors**

| | Strongly Agree (%) | Agree (%) | No Opinion (%) | Disagree (%) | Strongly Disagree (%) |
|---|---|---|---|---|---|
| 1. The tutoring helped the student I worked with. | 96 | 4 | | | |
| 2. The student I worked with learned content from me. | 83 | 17 | | | |
| 3. The student I worked with learned something about how to study | 65 | 35 | | | |
| 4. The student I worked with enjoyed being tutored. | 70 | 30 | | | |
| 5. I enjoyed tutoring. | 96 | 4 | | | |
| 6. When I learned content, I tutored better. | 87 | 9 | 4 | | |
| 7. I learned more about how to study and remember. | 65 | 22 | 13 | | |
| 8. The training sessions were generally helpful. | 65 | 22 | 13 | | |
| 9. Information about study strategies and how we remember was useful. | 61 | 39 | | | |
| 10. Information on how to tutor effectively was helpful. | 65 | 30 | 5 | | |
| 11. I would like to tutor again. | 100 | | | | |
| 12. I consider the person I tutored a friend. | 91 | | 9 | | |

# CHAPTER SEVEN

# Assessing Independent Learning Skills

If promoting independent learning skills in students is an important goal for classroom teachers, then assessing whether or not students acquire these skills becomes equally important. Perhaps the best way to show student skill development is to include evidence of strategic learning in student portfolios.

## STUDENT PORTFOLIOS IN THE EARLIER GRADES

A variety of performance assessments that demonstrate strategy use are appropriate. Many of the activities discussed in previous chapters lend themselves to products that can be placed in student portfolios. For example, teachers can tape younger students singing or reciting rhymes they have learned to help remember important information. Teachers can place the tapes in their students' portfolios. One elementary school invited parents to an end of the year performance, in which children sang songs and recited rhymes and told their parents the relationship between these activities and memory.

Teacher-completed checklists can also serve as documentation of progress toward independent learning in the early grades. Figure 7.1 contains an example of a checklist

designed for inclusion in student portfolios in kindergarten and first grade. Teachers in higher grades can easily adapt the learning outcomes included in Part I of this book as assessments for their students.

Examples of student-produced elaborative memory strategies and effective rehearsal routines can also form part of the portfolio. Sample card clusters, vocabulary and spelling study procedures, math problems and associated strategies, and study plans for upcoming tests demonstrate student progress in independent learning skills. Samples of students' notes and assignment books are also valid evidence of skill acquisition. Other evidence of organizational skills, such as student-made webs and diagrams, can show flexibility in summarizing and conceptualizing data in different types of ways.

# STUDENT PORTFOLIOS IN THE HIGHER GRADES

Products that show gradual improvement and reflect the student's growing ability to self-monitor and evaluate indicate an increase in skill development. Portfolios that include reviews of a peer's work (with the target student's name deleted) show the student's increasing skill as a peer editor or evaluator. As students mature, these skills should be reflected in revisions of their own work. Completed class participation monitoring sheets and self-evaluations also are legitimate and helpful contributions to student portfolios.

As students look toward graduation, their portfolios should reflect the development of a personal study style. By the senior year of high school, a student portfolio might include the following, which would indicate that he or she could be "certified" as an independent learner at graduation:

- a description of a favorite method for increasing comprehension skills while reading difficult text and a reflection on personal reading rate for varied reading material.

- an example of a study plan for a test or exam the student has developed, which might include a self-designed

# FIGURE 7.1
## Outcome Assessment
## Learning Strategies Curriculum
### (Kindergarten/ First Grade)

Student Name _____ Grade _____

Teacher _____ Date _____

B = Beginning skill level development
D = Developing skill level development
I = Independent skill level development

**Knowledge/Comprehension Outcomes**

1. ____ Student states, in his/her own words, that rhyming or music enhances retention (e.g., "making a song helps you remember").

2.____ Student states ways to help order and remember oral information in his/her own words, (e.g., "you should say what happened first, what happened second, or think of the picture the next day to remember the story").

3. ____ Student states that checking with a partner or self-evaluating his/her own work improves performance, (e.g., "you should check to see if your answers are right before you hand it in").

4. ____ Student identifies personalization as a memory/comprehension aid (e.g., "if you pretend you're in the story, it's easier to understand and remember").

5.____ Student identifies mental imagery as a memory aid (e.g., "making a picture in your mind helps you remember").

6. ____ Student states that finding similarities help you remember (e.g., "I remember that because it's the same as the first one we did").

7. ____ Student identifies rehearsal as a memory aid (e.g., "it helps you remember when you say it over and over").

*–continued*

## Application Outcomes

8. ____ Student has learned some content via rhythmic or musical means (e.g., alphabet, spelling of first or last name, days of the week, months, birthdate, address, numbers, or other _____).

9. ____ Student makes appropriate comment after listening to a story or teacher explanation.

10. ____ Student can repeat a comment made by a classmate after discussion.

11. ____ Student identifies a missing piece of information from a story or teacher explanation.

12. ____ Student accurately identifies important cues while listening (e.g., direction words, page numbers, due dates).

13. ____ Student evaluates own performance with a checksheet (accuracy not essential).

14. ____ Student successfully questions a partner after listening to or reading a story.

15. ____ Student formulates a question a teacher might ask about a story or lesson.

16. ____ Student demonstrates use of a verbal or visual prompt to aid memory (e.g., student circles an addition or subtraction sign to indicate computational operation).

17. ____ With teacher guidance, student successfully describes how class activities relate to his/her life.

18. ____ Student makes visual images of material to be remembered (e.g., draws pictures to represent spelling words).

19. ____ Student can organize information into a concept web with teacher guidance.

20. ____ Student uses effective rehearsal techniques with teacher guidance (e.g., copies whole word, checks for accuracy, rehearses both auditorily and visually, uses distributed practice).

# Figure 7.2
## School District's Goals for Increasing Academic Challenge and Independent Learning

### 1. Creating More Challenge Within the Regular Classroom

• What are the expectations for adequate progress?
• Should challenge be increased by deepening the scope of learning experience or by moving students further along the sequence?
• What classroom strategies create more challenge for individual students?

### 2. Giving Students the Skills for Academic Success

• How will students learn research skills, listening and note-taking skills, collaborative work skills?
• How will new cognitive skills such as analysis and synthesis abilities be fostered?
• How will problem-solving skills be incorporated into the curriculum?
• How will competency in the basics be assured?
• How will students become independent learners?

### 3. Meeting the Needs of All Students

• How will all students reach their potential?
• How will students learn to value learning (to become task rather than ego involved)?
• How can goal-setting conferences work for each student?
• How can all skills levels be met within the classroom?
• How can students develop personal interests and projects?
• How can students be motivated to learn?

### Other Questions for Discussion

• What role does homework play in academic success?
• What role does parent-school communication have in fostering academic achievement?

review sheet, card clusters for distributed review, a self-test, and sample pages from his or her notebook that indicate organization and elaboration.

- a description of a favorite problem-solving strategy and at least two "back up" strategies, along with examples showing how the student has used each strategy to solve a problem.

- a list of at least five different types of mnemonic devices or memory aids (such as acrostics or anagrams) and their definitions in the student's own words, along with student-generated examples of each type.

- examples of self-monitoring and self-evaluation using checksheets or reflections on his or her work.

## SUMMARY

Strengthening independent learning skills is not just for students who have special needs or require remedial learning. Rather, goals for the development of these skills can and should be embedded in a broader plan to increase academic challenge for *all* students. Figure 7.2 shows one school district's goals for enhancing skill development in its students. Strategic learning and study skills development are inherently related to academic challenge. The questions posed in Figure 7.2 srepresent a starting point for educators to embed independent learning skills across the curriculum from kindergarten through grade twelve.

Unless all teachers in every grade foster independent learning skills across content areas, it is unlikely that all students will develop them. As teachers and other members of school instructional support teams, we must challenge ourselves to inspire independent learning in our students so they can continue the process of lifelong learning.

# Appendices

# Metacognitive Interview

Appendix A contains the **Metacognitive Interview**, a tool for assessing the sophistication of students' understanding of strategic learning memories and an indicator of overall metacognitive maturity. While the interview has been successfully administered to children as young as third grade, it is best suited for students in grades five and above. When administered in a one-on-one situation, the interview can be given orally. It can also be given to an entire class at one time. In this case, the examiner should read both the questions and answer choices aloud to avoid any problems that might be caused because some students are poor readers. Students can then circle the letter of the response that they choose.

Also included in this appendix are **Scoring Directions**, a **Student Profile** sheet, and an **Intervention Plan**. The Metacognitive Interview may be scored by following the directions in the scoring guide and matching the descriptor numbers to those on the profile sheet. The Intervention Form can be highlighted to create an individualized intervention program for each student. Chapter 5 describes the use of the Metacognitive Interview and includes several case studies.

*Developed by Mary Ann Rafoth, Ph.D., and Linda Leal, Ph.D.*

# METACOGNITIVE INTERVIEW

The interview takes about 20 minutes to administer and consists of three parts: Metacognitive Knowledge, Metacognitive Skills and Strategies, and Monitoring and Self-Awareness.

Student _____

Grade _____ Age_____

School _____

Teacher _____

*General Directions:* Please respond honestly to all the questions below. The point of this exercise is to find out what you know about good study habits so your teachers can help you study better. Do not be concerned about whether or not your answers are right or wrong. You will not receive a grade on this assignment.

## I. Metacognitive Knowledge

**INSTRUCTIONS:** Below are some descriptions of situations in which a student is asked about memory activities. Please read each description, and think about how *you* would answer the question. Read the four answers labeled "A," "B," "C," and "D." Choose the response that best fits how *you* would answer the question.

1. One day two friends went to a birthday party and they met eight children they didn't know before. I'll tell you the names of the children they met: Bill, Jake, Jane, Sally, Anthony, Jim, Luis, and Cindy. After the party one friend went home and the other went to practice a play that he was going to be in. At the play practice, he met seven other children he did not know before, and their names were: Sally,

Anita, David, Maria, Jim, Dan, and Jake. At dinner that night, both children's parents asked them the names of the children they met at the **birthday party** that day. Which friend do you think remembered the most, the one who went home after the party, or the one who went to play practice where he met some more children? Why?

A. The one who went straight home would remember more, but I don't know why.

B. The one who went to the play would remember more, because some of the children at the play had the same names as those at the party, so it would remind him.

C. They would be able to remember both equally well.

D. The one who went straight home would remember more, because he wouldn't get mixed up by hearing all the other names of the children at the play.

2. If you wanted to phone your friend and someone told you the phone number, would it make any difference if you called right after you heard the number or if you got a drink of water first? Why?

A. It would help to get the drink because you would have more time to remember the number.

B. It wouldn't make any difference whether you called right away or got a drink first.

C. It would be better if you phoned first, but I don't know why.

D. You should phone first; otherwise, you might forget the number while you went to get a drink.

3. You are asked to remember a list of 10 numbers in

order. You are also asked to predict how many numbers in the sequence you will accurately remember immediately after the presentation of the numbers:

A. I can remember all 10—no problem.

B. I won't be able to remember all 10, but maybe about 6 or 7.

C. I can probably remember the first 2 numbers.

D. I'm not good at remembering numbers, and I won't remember any of them.

4. If you were trying to remember 10 numbers, as in the question above, which of the following ways do you think would be the best?

A. Say all of the numbers as quickly as possible.

B. Repeat the numbers over and over.

C. Try to put the numbers in groups to make it easier.

D. Try to think of another number, like an address or locker number, that is the same as some of the numbers.

5. The other day I played a tape for a girl. I asked her to listen carefully to the tape as many times as she wanted so she could tell me the story later. Before she began to listen to the tape, she asked me one question: "Am I supposed to remember the story word for word, just like on the tape, or can I tell you in my own words?" Which would be easier for her to do—learn the story word for word, or in her own words? Why?

A. Either way would be just as easy.
B. It would be easier for her to learn to say it in her

own words, because she could just explain the general idea. If she had to do it word for word, she might forget some of the words and that would ruin the whole story.

C. It would be easier for her to learn to say it word for word, because she would listen to each of the words on the tape very carefully.

D. It would be easier for her to learn to say it in her own words, but I don't know why.

6. Look at these two word lists:

List A: Mary-walk
Charley-jump
Joe-climb
Anne-sit

List B: boy-girl
hard-easy
cry-laugh
black-white

Suppose I showed you the two lists of words above (List A and List B) and asked you to learn them so that when I show you one of the words, you can tell me the other word that goes with it. For example, when I show you "boy," you would tell me "girl." Do you think one of these lists would be easier to learn than the other one? Why?

A. No. Both lists would be equally difficult to learn.

B. List B would be easier to learn because it is more meaningful.

C. List B would be easier to learn, but I'm not sure why.

D. List A would be easier to learn because the names might remind you of a few friends you have.

7. Jenna skimmed through a chapter in her science book before reading it. Juan started reading immediately. Which student will better remember what was read? Why?

   A. Jenna will remember more because she knew what the chapter was about before she read it.

   B. Juan will remember more because he didn't waste time and started reading right away.

   C. Jenna and Juan will remember the same amount.

   D. Jenna should remember more, but I don't know why.

8. Andrew likes to mark important things in his book with a yellow marker when he is reading. Susan does this, too. She marks everything, sometimes whole paragraphs. Andrew only marks main ideas and important words. Who will remember more? Why?

   A. Susan will remember more because she marked more information.

   B. They'll both remember the same amount.

   C. Andrew will remember more because he only marked what he wanted to remember.

   D. Andrew will remember more, but I'm not sure why.

## II. Metacognitive Skills and Strategies

**INSTRUCTIONS:** Below are some descriptions of situations in which a student is asked about memory activities. Please read each description and think about how you would study in that particular situation. Read the four answers: "A," "B," "C," and "D." Choose the one that is most like what *you* would do.

9. A student in class is told to read and study a section from one of the class' books. The student is told that he/she will be quizzed on the material. **If it were I:**

   A.  I would read the story and take notes by writing important points of the story.

   B.  I would read the story and try to put it in my own words.

   C.  I would read the story once.

   D.  I would read the entire story twice.

10. The teacher is introducing a new lesson. She writes some key words on the board and tells students what they mean. She also talks about the topic and tells the students some information. **If it were I:**

   A.  I would copy the key words down.

   B.  I would copy the key words down and try to write the definitions the teacher gave next to them.

   C.  I wouldn't write anything down—I'll remember it or wait for a review sheet.

   D.  I would copy the words and definitions and try to write down the main ideas the teacher was saying as well.

11. A student is shown a set of pictures of common objects arranged in a row on cards like those shown below. The goal of the task is for the student to recite the list of pictures in order, from left to right, when the pictures are no longer in view. The student is given two minutes to study the pictures, and his or her study behavior is observed. How much the student remembers is checked at the end of the two-minute period. **If it were I::**

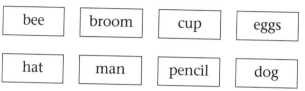

A. I would say the names of the pictures one at a time, repeating each label five times in a row. Rehearsal would sound like this, "Bee, bee, bee, bee, bee, broom, broom, etc."

B. I would say the names of the pictures consecutively, from left to right, first while looking at the pictures and then with my eyes turned away. Rehearsal would sound like this, "Bee, broom, cup, eggs, hat, man, etc."

C. I would look carefully at each of the pictures and try not to be distracted from the task during the two-minute period.

D. I would look at the pictures at the start of the study period but get distracted by other things in the room for most of the time.

**12.** A student is shown a set of pictures of common objects, arranged on cards in a random display like those shown below. The student is told that he or she should learn the names of the cards, in order to repeat them from memory. The cards can be recalled in any order that the student wants to use. The student is given three minutes to study the pictures. How much he or she remembers is checked at the end of the three-minute study period. **If it were I:**

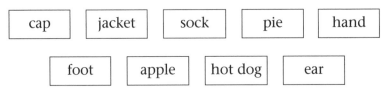

A. I would look at the pictures intently and try not to be distracted from the task during the time period.

B. I would say the names of the pictures over and over to myself, while looking at each in turn.

C. I would sort the items into categories of related things (food, clothing, and body parts) and study them in these sets.

D. I would move some items to put them in pairs with others (grouping, for example, sock and foot, hand and hot dog) but leave other pictures unsorted.

**13.** Suppose the student received a task just like the last task described above, but with one change in the instructions. Now the student is asked to study the items as long as he or she wants to, and to indicate when he or she knows them by ringing a bell. When the bell is rung, the teacher will ask the student to recall the items seen. **If it were I:**

A. I would look at and say each item just one time and then would ring the bell and say the items as quickly as possible.

B. I would look at some of the items, and then ring the bell.

C. I would say each item to myself a fixed number of times (e.g., three times, five times) and then ring the bell.

D. After studying, I would give myself a little "test" to see if I knew all of the items. When I could say them correctly in practice, I would ring the bell.

## III. Monitoring and Self-Awareness

**INSTRUCTIONS:** Below are some brief descriptions of some kinds of understandings a student might have about memory. Read each description and try to decide if the statement is true or false for you most of the time.

(Examiners should read each statement aloud.)

14. T  F  I can tell if one way to study something is better than another way.

15. T  F  I usually divide my study time so that easier things are studied for a longer time than are harder things.

16. T  F  I can tell when I know something and don't need to study it any longer.

17. T  F  Sometimes I know I know something, but I just can't think of it.

18. T  F  I usually cannot tell how well I will do on an exam.

19. T  F  I do different things when the teacher says to "remember" something than when he or she just says to "look it over."

20. T   F   I usually do not know if I've answered a test question correctly or not.

21. T   F   When I decide how long to study I think about the kind of stuff I have to remember and the kind of test I'm going to have.

22. T   F   Sometimes I get the feeling that I don't understand what I am reading.

23. T   F   I go over difficult material until I understand it better when reading or studying.

24. T   F   When I work out math problems, I try to make a good guess at what the answer should be, so I can compare my answer after I work the problem.

25. T   F   When I study for a test, I never think of questions the teacher might ask.

# METACOGNITIVE INTERVIEW SCORING DIRECTIONS

*Use in connection with the Metacognitive Student Profile, which immediately follows.*

Descriptors:            Directions for Scoring:

1.      If answers "D" on questions 1 and 2, mark "<u>yes</u>" for #1

        If answers "D" on only one or answers "A" on question 1 or "C" on question 2, mark "<u>emerging</u>"

        If answers "B" or "C" on question 1 and "A" or "B" on question 2, mark "<u>no</u>"

2.      If answers "B" on question 3, mark "<u>yes</u>" for #2

If answers "A" on question 3, mark "emerging"

If answers "C" or "D" on question 3, mark "no"

3. If answers "C" or "D" on question 4, mark "yes" for #3

If answers "B" on question 4, mark "emerging"

If answers "A" on question 4, mark "no"

4. If answers "B" on question 5, mark "yes" for #4

If answers "D" on question 5, mark "emerging"

If answers "A" or "C" on question 5, mark "no"

5. If answers "B" on question 6, mark "yes" for #5

If answers "C" on question 6, mark "emerging"

If answers "A" or "D" on question 6, mark "no"

6. If answers "A" on question 7, mark "yes" for #6

If answers "D" on question 7, mark "emerging"

If answers "B" or "C" on question 7, mark "no"

7. If answers "C" on question 8, mark "yes" for #7

If answers "D" on question 8, mark "emerging"

If answers "A" or "B" on question 8, mark "no"

8. If answers "A" or "B" on question 9, mark "yes" for #8

   If answers "C" or "D" on question 9, mark "no"

   (There is no emerging answer for this question.)

9. If answers "D," "B," or "A" on question 9, mark "yes" for #9

   If answers "C" on question 9, mark "no"

   (There is no emerging answer for this question.)

10. If answers "D" on question 10, mark "yes" for #10

    If answers "A" or "B" on question 10, mark "emerging"

    If answers "C" on question 10, mark "no"

11. If answers "B" on question 11, mark "yes" for #11

    If answers "A" on question 11, mark "emerging"

    If answers "C" or "D" on question 11, mark "no"

12. If answers "C" on question 12, mark "yes"for #12

    If answers "D" on question 12, mark "emerging"

    If answers "A" or "B" on question 12, mark "no"

13. If answers "D" on question 13, mark "yes" for #13

    If answers "C" on question 13, mark "emerging"

If answers "A" or "B" on question 13, mark "no"

14. If answers "True" on question 14, mark "yes" for #14

If answers "False" on question 14, mark "no"

(There is no emerging answer for this question.)

15. If answers "False" on question 15 and "True" on question 21, mark "yes" for #15

If answers "True" on both or "False" on both, mark "emerging"

If answers "True" on question 15 and "False" on question 21, mark "no"

16. If answers "True" on questions 16 and 17, mark "yes" for #16

If answers "True" on only one, mark "emerging"

If answers "False" on both questions 16 and 17, mark "no"

17. If answers "False" on questions 18 and 20, mark "yes" for #17

If answers "True" on one, mark "emerging"

If answers "True" on both questions 18 and 20, mark "no"

18. If answers "True" on questions 19 and 21, mark "yes" for #18

If answers "True" on only one, mark "emerging"

If answers "False" on both questions 19 and 21, mark "no"

19. If answers "True" on questions 22 and 23, mark "yes" for #19

If answers "True" on only one, mark "emerging"

If answers "False" on both questions 22 and 23, mark "no"

20.    If answers "True" on question 24 and "False" on question 25, mark "<u>yes</u>" for #20

If answers "True" on both or "False" on both, mark "<u>emerging</u>"

If answers "False" on question 24 and "True" on question 25, mark "<u>no</u>"

# METACOGNITIVE STUDENT PROFILE

| Metacognitive Knowledge: | Yes | Emerging | No |
|---|---|---|---|
| 1. Understands interference | ____ | ____ | ____ |
| 2. Knows limits of short term memory | ____ | ____ | ____ |
| 3. Knows effective aids to memorization | ____ | ____ | ____ |
| 4. Understands recall of meaningful material (gist vs. verbatim) | ____ | ____ | ____ |
| 5. Understands that meaning increases ease of rote memory | ____ | ____ | ____ |
| 6. Understands that preview increases comprehension | ____ | ____ | ____ |
| 7. Understands that directing attention to key information increases retention | ____ | ____ | ____ |

| Metacognitive Skills and Strategies: | Yes | Emerging | No |
|---|---|---|---|
| 8. Paraphrases information to aid recall in reading comprehension | ____ | ____ | ____ |
| 9. Uses repetition to aid comprehension and memory | ____ | ____ | ____ |
| 10. Uses notes as external aids for recall | ____ | ____ | ____ |
| 11. Uses rehearsal effectively | ____ | ____ | ____ |

12. Uses categorization/chunking strategies      _____ _____ _____

13. Self-tests while studying      _____ _____ _____

Monitoring and Self-Awareness:

14. Varies study techniques to meet task demands      _____ _____ _____

15. Divides study time effectively      _____ _____ _____

16. Has a sense of metacognitive awareness (knowing you know)      _____ _____ _____

17. Predicts exam grades successfully      _____ _____ _____

18. Directs self to perform learning strategies      _____ _____ _____

19. Senses poor comprehension and reviews material      _____ _____ _____

20. Uses estimation/prediction to monitor performance      _____ _____ _____

# INTERVENTION PLAN

*Use the results of the Student Profile to fill in the following form. Use a highlighter or another method to indicate suggested interventions for those answers that fall into the "emerging" or "no" categories.*

Student Name_____

Grade _____ Date _____

The areas in which this student is weak are indicated with highlighting. Suggestions for intervention follow.

## Metacognitive Knowledge

1. *Does not understand interference:*

Explain the concept of interference in memory. Provide

examples from the student's classroom that illustrate how interference reduces memory.

2. *Does not know limits of short-term memory:*

Explain that our memory can hold about seven (give or take two) units of meaningful information. Relate this to the seven-digit telephone number, the nine-digit social security number, and the five-digit zip code. There's a reason commonly used numbers fit within this range! Point out that the extended zip code numbers have not caught on because they exceed the limits of short-term memory.

3. *Does not know effective aids to memorization:*

Explain efficient rehearsal techniques (rehearse in the manner in which something is to be recalled, group or chunk material to be rehearsed, make associations with known material and rehearse the association). Provide examples from the student's current classwork that illustrate these points.

4. *Does not understand that remembering the gist is easier than verbatim recall:*

Explain how the brain works naturally to abstract out main ideas and themes from what we see, read, and hear. Provide examples from the student's daily life (using popular movies or recent class discussions, for example). Illustrate your point with a practice exercise asking the student to remember the main idea of a paragraph and then a verbatim recall of another paragraph.

5. *Does not understand that meaning increases ease of rote memory:*

Explain that our brain remembers information by association or linking. We link new information to old information. Thus, information that is naturally related in a meaningful way is automatically and easily remembered. Demonstrate with two work lists—one opposites, the other unrelated. Ask students to remember each list and compare the results.

6. *Does not understand that preview increases comprehension:*

Review the steps to the comprehension process (preview, active reading, summary or paraphrase, and review). Discuss how skimming something before reading is akin to getting to open the lid of a box and looking inside rather than just making a guess about its contents. Which method is most likely to produce an accurate answer? Previewing increases comprehension by letting you know "what's inside" before you read. You might need to use an actual box!

7. *Does not understand that directing attention to key information increases comprehension:*

Explain that making decisions about whether something is important or not increases remembering. When a reader decides to highlight particular information, that decision helps make that information "stick" in the brain. If you highlight too much, you have made no decisions and memory isn't enhanced. Demonstrate this with two readings about two pages long. Ask the student to highlight key ideas in one, but whole paragraphs in the other. Then, have the student compare recall of both stories.

## Metacognitive Skills and Strategies

8. *Does not paraphrase information to increase meaning and retention:*

Explain that meaningfulness controls remembering. If it makes sense to us, we can remember it fairly easily. Demonstrate by comparing understanding and retention for word definitions that are learned verbatim rather than through paraphrase.

9. *Does not use repetition to aid memory or use rehearsal effectively:*

Review effective rehearsal strategies and demonstrate student efficacy of different approaches with actual classroom material.

10. *Does not use notes as external aids for recall:*

Explain that taking notes in your own words increases

immediate comprehension and copying information from the board or overhead gives a student material to review later. Demonstrate several note-taking methods—mapping, outline, or split-page methods—for example. Provide feedback to students on the quality of their notes. Review elaboration of notes and provide feedback to students who have highlighted their notes, made clarifications, or added examples. Partner checks can be utilized to reduce teacher time. Compare test grades with and without appropriate notes to demonstrate efficacy with students.

11. *Does not use categorization or chunking strategies:*
Explain how categorization and chunking enhance memory—have the student test him/herself with and without chunking using actual classroom assignments.

12. *Does not self-test while studying:*
Ask the student how a teacher knows when a student has learned information. Suggest that the student could also give him/herself a little test to know when studying and learning were complete. Discuss how reviewing something a fixed number of times may cause the student to study too little or more than needed.

## Monitoring and Self-Awareness

13. *Does not vary study techniques to meet task demands or divide study time effectively:*
Discuss different approaches for different study tasks. Have student number homework from easiest to hardest and estimate the amount of time and type of approach necessary for each task. Record actual time spent and activity used to study. Compare actual and predicted.

14. *Does not predict exam grades successfully:*
Have the student make a chart for upcoming or regularly occurring tests and quizzes and predict his/her grade prior to each evaluation; record actual grade and compare. Discuss how self-testing can contribute to accurate prediction.

### 15. *Does not have a sense of metacognitive awareness:*

Discuss the "tip of the tongue" phenomena. Has this ever happened to the student? Rate homework and classwork assignments from hardest to easiest. Discuss why the student judged one class harder than another.

### 16. *Does not direct self to perform learning strategies:*

Discuss different types of strategies for learning (such as mnemonics and other elaborative strategies, organizational and chunking strategies, affective strategies, and rehearsal). Using the student's classwork, demonstrate a variety of strategies to enhance learning. Ask the student to choose his or her most difficult subject and help them apply strategies. Evaluate their success on the next quiz or test.

### 17. *Does not sense poor comprehension and reviews material:*

Review the steps in the comprehension process: preview, active reading (do I understand the content?), summary or paraphrase, and review. Practice "comprehension checks" during free reading with a timer. When the timer rings, student should record whether or not he or she understands what's being read. If the answer is no, students should review the material using steps above with a partner.

### 18. *Does not use estimation or prediction to monitor performance:*

Practice estimation and prediction with actual class material. Show that estimation in math and prediction in reading increase accuracy and comprehension. Students should articulate the common purposes of estimation and prediction.

# Study Skills Interview

Appendix B contains the **Study Skills Interview** and **Student Profile**. The Study Skills Interview is used to obtain specific information about how a student studies for current coursework and tests. While it has been successfully given to children as young as third grade, it is best suited for students in grades five and above. The subject areas listed on these two forms can be modified to reflect the subjects students are actually taking at the time of the interview. When administered in a one-on-one situation, it can be given orally with the examiner recording student responses. It can also be administered to an entire class by allowing students to write their responses in the blanks provided.

The Student Profile is used to summarize the information from the Study Skills Interview and requires the examiner to rate the efficiency of the student's skills by subject area and identify potential strategies for improvement. Chapter 5 discusses the use of the Study Skills Interview and includes several case studies.

*Developed by Mary Ann Rafoth, Ph.D.*

# STUDY SKILLS INTERVIEW

Student Name _____

Grade _____        Age_____

Teacher _____

Please answer the following questions as completely and honestly as you can. Your answers will point out ways to help you study more easily and effectively.

**1. How do you study for the following kinds of tests?**

A) Spelling _____
_____
_____
_____

How often are you tested?
_____

Are you tested on the spelling of the words only or on the definitions of the words as well?
_____

Have your teachers or parents suggested different ways to study to you?
_____
_____

B) History/Social Studies
_____
_____
_____

How often are you tested?
_____

What type of tests are you given (short answer, fill in the blank, true-false, multiple choice)?

_____

_____

_____

How do you study in class? (for example, do you take notes? copy from the board? try to remember what the teacher is saying?)

_____

_____

C) Science

_____

_____

_____

How often are you tested?

_____

What type of tests are you given?

_____

How do you study in class?

_____

D) Math

_____

_____

_____

How often are you tested?

_____

What type of tests are you given (computation, story problems, timed tests)?

_____

_____

_____

2. **What is the hardest subject for you to learn right now?**

_____

_____

_____

What is your usual grade?

_____

How do you currently study for tests?

_____

_____

_____

How often are you tested in this area?

_____

3. **Do you usually study only the night before a test or a little each night after your other homework is completed?**

_____

_____

_____

# STUDY SKILLS PROFILE

For each subject, rank the student's study skills from 1 (inefficient) to 5 (efficient). Underline or circle the specific recommendations that would benefit the student most.

Student _____

Grade _____     Age _____

Teacher _____

Date _____

## Strategy Use

| Subject Area | Inefficient   Efficient | Recommendation |
|---|---|---|
| Spelling | 1 2 3 4 5 | Self-test initially; eliminate knowns; analyze unknowns; rehearse and mnemonics; paired associate task; self-test |
| History/Social Studies | 1 2 3 4 5 | Incorporate SQ4R (Survey, Question, Read and Reflect, Recite, Review); make summary during "recite/reflect phase; apply mnemonics to info. on worksheets; review studying for and taking multiple choice, true-false, and fill-ins |
| Science | 1 2 3 4 5 | Incorporate SQ4R; note-taking strategies; studying fill-ins, multiple choice, true-false |
| Math | 1 2 3 4 5 | Work new practice problems and check; estimation strategies to check work |

| Hardest Subject | 1 2 3 4 5 | SQ4R; increase strategies for increasing text comprehension; test-taking strategies; mnemonics; note-taking skills |
| Distributed Study | 1 2 3 4 5 | Prior to test review for several nights; make study cards to review throughout day |

# Peer Tutoring Manual for the Share the Secret Program

Appendix C contains the **Peer Tutoring Manual** for the "Share the Secret" program. In the initial program, students identified as tutees were given the Metacognitive Interview so their tutors could use the suggested interventions on the Intervention Form to help improve tutees' study skills. To replicate the program, please use the Metacognitive Interview and Intervention Form provided in Appendix A to accomplish this step.

Appendix C also includes exercises and suggestions for training peer tutors. Chapter 6 discusses the peer training program in depth.

*Developed by Mary Ann Rafoth, Ph.D., and Brooke Yellets, M.Ed.*

# SHARE THE SECRET

The ability to learn independently—to organize time, structure your studies, use a variety of learning strategies to increase remembering and understanding—separates successful from unsuccessful students in the classroom to a greater degree than ability. These are the secrets of school success that need to be shared.

# HOW STUDENTS LEARN BEST

*Review and discuss the following items with peer tutors.*

Students Learn Best When...

1. They are actively involved.
2. They have concrete experiences.
3. They have options.
4. They are satisfying their own interests and needs.
5. They are accepted for their own learning styles and rates.
6. They are succeeding.
7. They have strong self-concepts as learners.
8. Their objectives are met.
9. They are self-motivated.

# YOUR JOB AS A TUTOR

1. Encourage your tutees by helping them to be right.
2. Let them know *when* they are right.
3. Help them realize *when* they have learned.
4. Help them realize *what* they have learned.
5. Help them realize what they *still need* to learn.

Adapted from Sabrinsky (1992).

# CHARACTERISTICS THAT LEAD TO SUCCESSFUL TUTORING

DIRECTIONS: List below in priority order from 1 to 15 the numbers of the characteristics that you think would be most important for successful tutoring.

| | | |
|---|---|---|
| _____ | 1. | ability to encourage |
| _____ | 2. | ability to be patient |
| _____ | 3. | ability to accept people as they are, where they are, and like them for it |
| _____ | 4. | ability to withhold personal opinion |
| _____ | 5. | ability to use good listening skills |
| _____ | 6. | ability to keep focus on academic tasks |
| _____ | 7. | ability to demonstrate a sense of humor |
| _____ | 8. | ability to admit mistakes |
| _____ | 9. | ability to be dependable/show up for sessions |
| _____ | 10. | ability to plan and be prepared |
| _____ | 11. | ability to respect and maintain privacy |
| _____ | 12. | ability to keep good records |
| _____ | 13. | ability to cooperate in the classroom |
| _____ | 14. | ability to deliver content information in a clear and understandable way |
| _____ | 15. | ability to share tips on "how to study" |

Adapted from Sabrinsky (1992).

# HOW TO BE AN EFFECTIVE TUTOR

1. Determine your own attitudes about school, teachers, and learning.
2. Get to know the students you are tutoring. Try to be informed about the interests of your tutees before you begin working with them.
3. Give the students you are tutoring your undivided attention.
4. Listen to your tutees.
5. Show trust, respect, and acceptance.
6. Be polite.
7. Build confidence whenever possible by recognizing small successes.
8. Learn the names and pronunciations of the students you are tutoring.
9. Be relaxed and friendly.
10. Clarify the purpose of tutoring.
11. Be prepared and prompt for each session.
12. Never let students reach the point of frustration.
13. Don't be afraid to make mistakes or say, "I don't know."
14. Keep records of the tutoring session.
15. Be a role model.
16. Ask for help when you need it.
17. Never criticize the supervising teacher or school rules.
18. Be enthusiastic.
19. Maintain confidentiality.
20. Respect the privacy of the student you are tutoring.

Adapted from Sabrinsky (1992).

# PLANNING YOUR FIRST MEETING

What will you do the first time you meet the student you are assigned to tutor? What will you want to know? What will you say?

Think about the following questions and respond to each one:

1. What do you want to know about the persons you will be tutoring? Is this the same kind of information they should know about you?

   Their names? Do they have nicknames? What would they like you to call them?

   What grades are they in?

   Have they always been in this school district?

   Do they have brothers or sisters?

   Other facts?

2. What will happen in the tutoring session? What do they need to bring? How should they prepare?

3. What subjects are the hardest for them? What do they want help with the most?

4. What will you say if they ask why you volunteered to tutor?

5. Write out your opening comments. How will you begin the first meeting?

   "Hi, I'm...."

# GUIDELINES FOR PREPARING FOR A TEST

1. **Know when the test will be given**—what date, time, etc. Will you have the entire class period to complete the exam or will it be given at the beginning or end of class? Will this be a timed test?

2. **Know what the test will cover**—what chapters, what notes, etc. Will there be questions asking you to apply information to new situations not specifically discussed in class or in your textbook?

3. **Know your teacher.** Will your teacher give detailed questions about specific dates, numbers, distances, or names? Will your teacher allow you to ask questions about words you do not understand or ways to interpret a question? Will your teacher allow you to use external aids such as dictionaries, tables, and calculators while taking the test? Ask your teacher about these and other concerns *before* the test.

4. **Know what kinds of test you will be taking.** Will there be fill-in-the-blank, completion, essay, multiple-choice, or true-false questions?

5. **Know how to study.** Which study methods will work best for the material you need to learn and the type of test you will be given? Plan your study ahead of time so you will have ample opportunity to learn all the material. Do *not* engage in last minute cramming. Ask your teacher for suggestions concerning how to study. While studying, predict material or questions that are likely to be on the test.

6. **Know yourself.** What are your test-taking strengths and weaknesses? What type of question is most difficult for you? What type of material is most difficult for you to study? Plan methods you can use to overcome your weaknesses and capitalize on your strengths. Ask your teacher for suggestions. Also, rest, proper nutrition, and exercise are important for good test performance.

6. **Know how to take a test.** See "Guidelines for Taking a Test" to review techniques.

Adapted from Rafoth, Leal, and DeFabo (1993).

# GUIDELINES FOR TAKING A TEST

1. **Take time to read test directions** carefully before answering the questions. Watch for changes in directions.

2. **Skim or look over the entire test** before you begin answering individual questions.

3. **Do not read more into a question** than is actually there.

4. Place a question mark in front of any questions you are uncertain about rather than spend too much time deliberating over it and becoming frustrated. Return to this question after you have answered the other questions. Eliminate the obvious incorrect answers when responding to multiple-choice questions.

5. **Underline key words** in items that are difficult to answer.

6. **Read all choices** before making a selection on a multiple-choice exam.

7. **Look for absolute words** such as "all," "none," "never," "always,"; keep in mind there are not many absolutes in our world.

8. **All parts of a true-false question** must be true before the statement can be true.

9. **When matching**, first answer items that you know, and then go back to remaining items and make the best choice.

10. **If you have time**, go back and reconsider your answers. Always proofread your test before turning it in.

11. **Never change an answer** unless you understand clearly why you are doing so.

12. **Ignore the pace** of other students.

Adapted from Schilling (1984).

# TEST YOURSELF ON TAKING TESTS

*Do this with peer tutors after reviewing the guidelines for preparing for and taking a test. Tutors should repeat the exercise with tutees.*

Mark true or false:

_____ 1. Always mark true if the question includes "never."

_____ 2. Look over the questions first, read directions if you have time.

_____ 3. Don't just read the question. Try to imagine what the teacher meant by the question.

_____ 4. Underline key words to help you focus on the question.

_____ 5. Mark an answer as soon as it looks like the right one to you when taking a multiple-choice test.

_____ 6. All parts of a True-False must be true for the statement to be true.

_____ 7. Never double-check your test before turning it in.

_____ 8. Check to see how quickly other students are going and adjust your pace to their pace.

_____ 9. Never change an answer unless you know you're wrong.

_____ 10. Skip over questions you're unsure of and come back to them later.

(Correct Answers: F  F  T  T  F  T  F  F  T  T)

# STRATEGIC STUDY SHEET (SSS)

| List Classes Here | Current Grades for Each Type of Classwork (quizzes, labs, homework, exams) | Brainstorm and Study Strategies for Each Weak Area | Progress Report | Agreed upon Reward* |
|---|---|---|---|---|
|  |  |  |  |  |
|  |  |  |  |  |
|  |  |  |  |  |
|  |  |  |  |  |
|  |  |  |  |  |
|  |  |  |  |  |
|  |  |  |  |  |

*Rewards could be something the tutee gives him or herself or something agreed upon by the tutor and tutee, such as five minutes of conversation instead of tutoring in a given session.

# EXERCISE 1: WOULD A GOOD TUTOR SAY THIS?

*Why or why not? Respond and discuss.*

1. These problems are all wrong. Let me show you the right way.

2. I agree that your teacher isn't fair.

3. You started off correctly with that problem. Can you tell me what you were thinking when you worked the problem?

4. Your handwriting is so bad that I can't begin to read it.

5. Overall, this page looks good. Were you saying that it's wrong to use animals for experiments in your essay? Can you put the reasons you think this is true in your essay, too?

6. Let me read your paper aloud. Tell me what you like best about it.

7. Okay, I read your paper. Let me tell you how to fix it. You've got spelling mistakes. I'll correct those while you work on math.

8. If you're having a test on history, I'll tell you what to study. Give me your notes and I'll circle the stuff you should memorize.

9. What information did the teacher stress in class?

10. Before we start studying, how do you like to remember information? Have you ever made a picture in your head or a rhyme?

# EXERCISE 2: HOW WOULD A GOOD TUTOR RESPOND?

*How would you respond to these comments from students being tutored? Discuss your answers.*

1. You had this teacher before. What's on the test?

2. I just can't do math.

3. Read my paper and correct the errors you see in it.

4. I don't care about that class; it's stupid.

5. Why try? If the teacher doesn't like you, you'll get a low grade.

6. Why should I do homework if it's not graded?

7. I just can't remember all that information.

8. I think this paper is really good. I don't want to work on it anymore.

9. I don't really care about grades.

10. This is so hard. Can't you just tell me the answers?

# EXERCISE 3: SELF-EVALUATION FOR PEER TUTORS

*Complete after seven sessions.*

In my tutoring sessions I:

_____ come prepared.

_____ treat my tutee with respect.

_____ keep information confidential.

_____ encourage without providing answers.

_____ am aware of when my tutee is becoming frustrated.

_____ share tips on how to remember and study.

_____ try to stay focused on academic tasks.

_____ work in short, concentrated sessions.

_____ review frequently.

_____ let my tutee talk.

_____ provide constructive feedback.

_____ remind tutees to use strategies.

_____ help tutees make their lessons meaningful.

_____ praise success.

_____ reinforce effort.

# STRUCTURED INTERVIEW FOLLOWING PEER TUTORIAL

*Use this interview to collect evaluation information from students who have been tutored. These students tend to respond better in an interview than when completing a paper and pencil survey.*

Interviewee Name:_____

Age:_____

Grade:   9   10   11   12

Sex: ___ Male ___Female

## INTRODUCTION

Hi! Your school has asked me to talk with everyone who participated in the peer-tutoring program and who came to study skills lab. The teachers and administrators want to find out if it helped you. They want to know if they should do it again, change it to make it better, or choose not to do it next year. Your answers are important. Please be honest. I will write down your responses. When I have spoken with everyone, I will write a summary of the results for the school, but I will not say that a particular student said any particular thing. Your statements will remain confidential.

It will only take about 15 minutes.

1. How often do you come to the study skills lab?

2. What usually happens?

3. Did a student from the Peer Helping Club work with you during the fall?

___yes ___no

4. If so, what was his/her name? _____

5. How often did he/she work with you? _____

6. What did he/she help you with?

7. Did working with the peer tutor:
   SA = Strongly Agree
   A = Agree
   N/O = No Opinion
   D = Disagree
   SD = Strongly Disagree

|  | SA | A | N/O | D | SD |
|---|---|---|---|---|---|
| a. Help you understand your work? | — | — | — | — | — |
| b. Help you get your work done? | — | — | — | — | — |
| c. Help improve your grades on tests? | — | — | — | — | — |
| d. Help improve your overall grade? | — | — | — | — | — |
| e. Help you feel better about school? | — | — | — | — | — |
| f. Help you learn how to study? | — | — | — | — | — |
| g. Help you study for tests? | — | — | — | — | — |
| h. Help you with homework? | — | — | — | — | — |
| i. Do you consider the tutor to be a friend? | — | — | — | — | — |

8. If you were given the choice, would you like to work with a peer tutor again? Why or why not?

9. Has coming to the study skills lab:

a. Improved your grades?          ___yes ___no ___somewhat
b. Improved test scores?          ___yes ___no ___somewhat
c. Improved your attitude
   toward school?                 ___yes ___no ___somewhat
d. Improved your attendance?      ___yes ___no ___somewhat
e. Improved how you study?        ___yes ___no ___somewhat
f. Helped you make friends?       ___yes ___no ___somewhat

10. The best thing about the peer tutoring is:

11. The worst thing about the peer tutoring is:

12. How could this program be improved?

13. Given a choice, would you participate in this program again? Why or why not?

14. Do you think this program should be continued?

15. Name one thing you learned from your tutor or from the study skills lab.

16. Would you like to make any other comments about the program?

Thank you for talking with me!

# PEER TUTOR SURVEY

*Give this survey to students who served as peer tutors after the sessions have been completed.*

**PART I**

This year you participated in a peer-tutoring program. You also received training in how to help other students study more effectively and how to be a more effective tutor. We would like your opinion about the experience. Please be honest in your responses. Thank you for your help.

1. Did you tutor a student this semester?

    \_\_\_yes \_\_\_no

(If you did not tutor a student, hand in your survey now.)

2. How many students did you tutor? _____

3. On the average, how many times did you work with each student each week?

    \_\_\_ About once a week
    \_\_\_ About twice a week
    \_\_\_ About three to four times a week
    \_\_\_ Usually daily

4. On the average, how long were your sessions?

    \_\_\_ 15 minutes or less
    \_\_\_ About 30 minutes
    \_\_\_ Usually the entire period

5. Please estimate how much of your time each session was spent in going over content, helping with homework specifically, or discussing how to study, remember information, or prepare for a test.

    \_\_\_% Reviewing content
    \_\_\_% Helping with homework
    \_\_\_% How to study

6. How many of the training sessions did you attend?
___ All of all four
___ Parts of all four
___ All of three
___ All of one and parts of the others
___ One
___ None

## PART II

Please respond to the following statements using the scale below by placing a checkmark on the line:

SA = Strongly Agree
A = Agree
N/O = No Opinion
D = Disagree
SD = Strongly Disagree

|  | SA | A | N/O | D | SD |
|---|---|---|---|---|---|
| 1. The student I worked with was helped by the tutoring. | — | — | — | — | — |
| 2. The student I worked with learned content from me. | — | — | — | — | — |
| 3. The student I worked with learned something about how to study. | — | — | — | — | — |
| 4. The student I worked with enjoyed being tutored. | — | — | — | — | — |
| 5. I enjoyed tutoring. | — | — | — | — | — |
| 6. When I tutored, I improved my own content knowledge. | — | — | — | — |  |
| 7. I learned more about how to study and remember. | — | — | — | — | — |

8. The training sessions were
   generally helpful.      ___  ___  ___  ___  ___

9. Information about study
   strategies and how we
   remember was useful.    ___  ___  ___  ___  ___

10. Information on how to tutor
    effectively was helpful.  ___  ___  ___  ___  ___

11. I would like to tutor again.  ___  ___  ___  ___  ___

12. I consider the person I tutored
    a friend.               ___  ___  ___  ___  ___

**PART III**

Please answer the following questions as well as you can.
We need to know how to make the program better and
whether we should repeat the program next year.

1. What problems did you encounter tutoring? (For
example, was the student you worked with frequently
absent? Was the student unprepared for the tutoring session?)

2. What suggestions do you have to improve the program? How could it be a better experience for the students
you tutored and for you?

Thank You!

# Bibliography

Branscombe, N. A., Goswami, D., and Schwartz, J. 1992. *Students Teaching; Teachers Learning.* Portsmouth, NH: Boynton/Cook Heinemann.

Bretzing, B. H., Kulhavy, R. W., and Caterino, L. C. 1987. "Note-taking by Junior High Students." *Journal of Educational Research* 80: 359-62.

Bruning, R., Schraw, G., and Ronning, R. 1995. *Cognitive Psychology and Instruction.* Englewood Cliffs, NJ: Prentice Hall.

Flavell, J. H. 1992. "Perspectives on Perspective Taking." In *Piaget's Theory: Prospects and Possibilities.* Edited by H. Balin and P. Pufall, 107-139. Hillsdale, NJ: Lawrence Erlbaum.

Fitzpatrick, E. M. 1982. *Study Skills Program Level III.* Reston, VA: National Association of Secondary Principals.

Frender, G. 1990. *Learning to Learn.* Nashville, TN: Incentive Publications.

Gettinger, M. and Nicaise, M. 1997. "Study Skills." In *Children's Needs II.* Edited by G. Bear, K. Minke, and A. Thomas, 407-418. Bethesda, MD: National Association of School Psychologists.

Glenberg, A. and Epstein, W. 1987. "Inexpert Calibration of Comprehension." *Memory and Cognition* 15: 84-93.

Hallahan, D.P., Lloyd, J.W., Kauffman, J.M., and Loper, A. B. 1983. "Academic Problems." In *The Practice of Child Therapy*. Edited by R.J. Morris and T.R. Kratcochwill, 113-143. Elmsford, NY: Pergamon Press.

Hyerle, D. 1995. "Thinking Maps: Seeing is Understanding." *Educational Leadership* 53(4): 85-89.

Jones, C. H., Slate, J. R., Blake, P. C., and Holifield, S. D. 1992. "Two Investigations of the Academic Skills of Junior and Senior High School Students." *The High School Journal* 76 (1): 24-29.

Morris, C. C. 1990. "Retrieval Processes Underlying Confidence in Comprehension Judgements." *Journal of Experimental Psychology: Learning, Memory, and Cognition* 16: 223-232.

Palinscar, A. and Brown, A. 1984. "Reciprocal Teaching of Comprehension Fostering Strategies and Comprehension Monitoring Strategies." *Cognition and Instruction* 1(2): 117-175.

Presseisen, B.Z., Sternberg, R., Fischer, K.W., Knight, C.C., and Feverstein, R. 1990. *Learning and Thinking Styles: Classroom Interaction*. Washington, D.C.: National Education Association.

Pressley, M., Borkowski, J., and Schneider, W. 1987. "Cognitive Strategies: Good Strategy Users Coordinate Metacognition and Knowledge." In *Annals of Child Development*. Edited by R. Vasta and G. Whitehurst, 89-129. Greenwich, CT: JAI.

Rafoth, M. A. March 1995. "System-Wide Consultation in Learning Strategies: A Working Model in Three Districts." Presentation at the National Association of School Psychologists Conference in Chicago, IL.

Rafoth, M. A. March 1996. "Efficacy of a Peer Tutoring Program Incorporating Learning Strategies Training with High Risk Adolescents." Presentation at the National Association of School Psychologists Conference in Atlanta, GA.

Rafoth, M. A. April 1998. "A Tale of Three Teachers: Effective Instructional Consultation Using Study Skills and Metacognitive Assessment and Training." Presentation at the National Association of School Psychologists Conference in Orlando, FL.

Rafoth, M. A., Leal, L., and DeFabo, L. 1993. *Strategies for Learning and Remembering: Study Skills Across the Curriculum.* Washington, D.C.: National Education Association.

Sabrinsky, E. F. 1992. *Tutoring: Learning by Helping.* Rev. ed. Minneapolis, MN: Educational Media Corporation.

Schilling, F. C. 1984. "Teaching Study Skills in the Intermediate Grades—We Can Do More." *Journal of Reading* 28: 620-23.

Schneider, W. and Pressley, M. 1989. *Memory Development Between 2 and 20.* New York: Springer-Verlag.

Swanson, H. L. 1990. "Influence of Metacognitive Knowledge and Aptitude on Problem Solving." *Journal of Educational Psychology* 82: 306-314.

Weinstein, C. E., Zimmerman, S. A., and Palmer, D. R. 1988. "Assessing Learning Strategies: The Design and Development of the LASSI." In *Learning and Study Strategies.* Edited by C. E. Weinstein, E. Goetz, and P. Alexander, 25-40. San Diego: Academic Press Inc.

Winograd, R. N. 1984. "Strategic Difficulties in Summarizing Text." *Reading Research Quarterly* 14: 404-424.

---

# SOURCES FOR SONGS, RHYMES, AND OTHER MATERIALS

Rock 'n Learn. P.O. Box 3595, Conroe, TX 77305. (audiocassettes with books)

Totline Publications. Warren Publishing House, Inc., P.O. Box 2250, Everett, WA 98203. (books and classroom resources)

# About the Author

Mary Ann Rafoth, Ph.D., is a professor in the Educational and School Psychology Department of Indiana University of Pennsylvania (IUP), where she coordinates the School Psychology Certificate program and directs the department's Child Study Center. She earned her bachelor's degree in education at the Miami University of Ohio, and her master's degree in school psychometry and doctoral degree in educational psychology at the University of Georgia. She worked as a classroom teacher in Ohio and as a school psychologist in Georgia and Illinois. A frequent consultant to schools, Rafoth conducts research that involves strengthening independent learning skills in students, alternatives to retaining students, and school readiness issues. Her spouse, Ben, directs the Writing Center at IUP. They live in Indiana, PA, with their two children, Henry, 13, and Paige, 9.